STAIRWAY
FROM
HEAVEN

Stairway
from
Heaven

A DAUGHTER'S
UNDENIABLE PROOF
OF
LIFE AFTER LIFE

Shushana Castle

Dedicated to Mom,

this is for you.

Thanks for continuing to live up to your nickname,

Chaldean Commander-in-Chief Angel,

offering all these miracles—

thank you for making me the woman who I am

and

to Jack, Mom's prayers and mine were answered when we met,

words cannot describe my love for you

and

to Steve, who celebrated our parents

and took immaculate care of them

and

with love to Mom's loving parents,

Habbuba Sinawi Maizy

and Yousif Maizy

who gave life to twelve children, four of whom went to

heaven as children

and

to Mom's loving sisters and brothers,

Hassina Maizy Bahrou

Georgette Maizy Tobia

Samira Maizy Sinawi

Louis Yousif Maizy

George Yousif Maizy

Manuel Yousif Maizy

Samir Yousif Maizy

Contents

Introduction

My mother liked to tell me a story about when she was a little girl. She grew up in Baghdad, Iraq, where the summer midday heat reaches 120 degrees. At night, however, the air is cool, and she and her family, like the other residents of the city, would sleep in their beds under heavy duvets on the flat rooftops.

One evening, she climbed the stairs to the rooftop before the rest of her family arrived. She was crying, as she did almost every night. "I was a crybaby," she would say, and she'd tell me how as a girl she would cry for no reason, though she had been born into a loving, warm, responsive family. And there, alone beneath the stars, she was met by a spirit, an angel she said. It was powerful and strong, yet calming. The angel comforted her and spoke to her, saying, "Do not cry anymore. Everything is fine." My mother knew it was God talking to her, and she felt His peace. She said she never again cried without cause, and she felt the constant presence of God and her angel from a very young age, protecting her, guiding her.

This early experience was the starting point of Mom's personal relationship with God, building on the foundation her parents had already laid for her with their devotion to God and the Chaldean Catholic Church. She told me that from this time on, as a little girl she became fully immersed in her own passion for the glory of God, the saints, angels and the Catholic Church.

My whole life, I've marveled at my mother's excitement in being faithful and how miracles wove themselves through the fabric of her daily routines. Intuitions. Answered prayers. Healings. Signs. To her, these miracles were the natural outcome of a devoted life. To the hundreds of people she prayed for, counseled and mentored, these miracles brought blessings in union with God's truth.

Since Mom died in 2014, the miracles have kept coming—more than fifty strong, evidence-based miracles to date. They are proofs that there is life after life, invitations to deepen my own faith in God. The decision to share thirty-some here has been an evolution. Never in a hundred years did I think I would write a book about miracles, but my mother has guided me to share them. I am the deliverer, honoring the miracles, describing them in exact detail, precisely as they occurred and passing them on to you, but she is the one shaping the book.

As I witness these miracles, the ones you are about to read, I am both in awe and deeply appreciative. I become highly alert, then replay the scene immediately in my memory over and over. Every time I am stunned and grateful. By sharing these miracles with me, then guiding me to share them with you, my mother continues to communicate God's infinite love and unwavering presence, offering inspiration for those who may need guidance and faith, just as she did when she was on earth.

My mother, Mary Maizy Kherkher, was born in Baghdad, Iraq, on December 8, 1932. She was one of twelve children born to Habuba Sinawi and Yousif Maizy. Four brothers ascended into heaven during their childhood. Mom would tell me how her mom found ways to make each child feel exceptionally special, dedicating quality time to each one. And I know from my trips to Baghdad that my grandmother also had a fabulous sense of humor—she loved to laugh and make others laugh, too.

At the age of twenty-one, Mom left her family to go to college in America, arriving with absolutely nothing because at the port in Philadelphia, she watched her luggage drop into the ocean as it was being unloaded from the ship. She said it was mostly filled with beautiful gifts and gold for the family here, plus her most special dresses. It was never recovered.

She attended Wayne State University in Michigan and studied math and psychology. Though she never intended to stay in America, she met my father, Razouk Mansour Kherkher. She fell in love with his devotion to God, his sincerity and his respect for her. They married in 1958.

My parents shared strong cultural values and backgrounds. Both were Chaldean—in Mesopotamia, during the time of Jesus,

Mesopotamia was divided into Chaldea, Assyriana and Babylonia, today's Iraq and greater area. And though they both spoke fluent Arabic and English, they both shared Aramaic as a native tongue, the language that Jesus spoke (in addition to Hebrew). When Jesus died on the cross, His mother and the Romans at His feet, it was in Aramaic that He called out to His father. These common links to language, land and culture were a large part of my parents' union, and they shared it with my brother and I, speaking Aramaic in our home. In our late teens—the after-school sports years—English became more prominent, but the Aramaic never disappeared.

Soon after Mom and Dad were married, they moved to Los Angeles, in part to be closer to Mom's brother George, who had moved there. I was born there in 1960, and two years later my brother Steven was born. Then in 1965, Mom and Dad moved to Houston because my father's brother, Louis, convinced them to make Houston their home. It is there that she called home for the next forty-nine years—the rest of her life.

There was no Chaldean Catholic Church in Houston, so my parents joined the Roman Catholic Church. Both served the Holy Eucharist on Sundays and were devoted to daily prayer and public charity.

Mom's commitment to God informed everything she did. She would say she wanted to serve as Saint Theresa of Calcutta did, giving her life to helping others, and Mom understood her own calling was to serve right where she lived. For thirty years, she volunteered at

St. Luke's and Methodist hospitals where she served many thousands and thousands of hours as a language interpreter and spiritual advisor to doctors and patients.

Hundreds of people were attracted to her for advice, seeking her wisdom. She loved to pray for others. Her morning and nightly prayers to Mother Mary, Jesus, God and her favorite saints were for her long list of family, friends and strangers—anyone in need of God's guidance. Ask and you shall receive, says the Bible, and Mom felt very comfortable following through with the asking. She took intense notice to the answers to her prayers and the spiritual signs she would receive. I was always captivated by her ultimate devotion and grace, her deep satisfaction in communicating with God and offering counsel based on God's responses.

Mom also took huge pleasure in sharing her feasts of gourmet Middle Eastern cuisine, bringing people together around her table. Everyone was welcome. The broken. The neglected. The lonely. World leaders. My brother's entire college football team. Doctors. Patients and their families. Regardless of faith, political affiliation or philosophical standing, everyone was warmly welcome at the same table. In fact, they were drawn to it. People could sense that her home was a place of laughter, prayer and lots of food. These feasts happened frequently as I was growing up and continued until the last year she walked the earth. Even as she prepared and served these feasts, she was ever casual and relaxed. That was her style. She also loved telling corny jokes, including ones about getting to heaven.

Mom was exceedingly humble, shy even, about these gifts she shared. Hers was a gospel of love. "Love is the answer to everything," she'd say. "When you ask questions of life, if you include love and compassion, it will be the right answer." I believe that her life of boundless love, her devotion to God, and her selfless service and generosity were the foundation for a life abundant with miracles—a life that continues.

She walked her talk, teaching forgiveness, compassion, kindness, modesty and patience through her example. Every word she spoke came from all-encompassing love—it was always love rolling off her tongue. She never spoke in the negative. In fact, my brother Steve and I were not allowed to use the word "no" in our home growing up.

And so it is that I am still saying yes. Yes to miracles. Yes to my mother showing up in astonishing ways. Yes to writing a book I never dreamed of writing. Yes to God and yes to faith.

Miracles, they are everywhere. Tap into them. Sometimes, the evidence is right in front of us.

Just Breathe

This night in Colorado I lie in bed in a state of alarmed aware-ness. My concentration is in every motion of my breath. I feel my lungs open up, and I'm in tune with every oxygen and hydrogen molecule entering my lungs, aware as they transport life support to every cell in my body.

Earlier this afternoon I had a nice conversation with Mom and told her Jack and I were going out for an early dinner. We returned home about seven o'clock at night.

But since we've been home, something has taken over me. Rather than enjoying the outdoors as I usually do in the evening, I want to be in bed, my head comfortable on the pillow.

My focus is on survival of all functions in every molecule in my body. I do not want to be anywhere else. There is a sense of urgency and stillness. Breathing is an effort. I have to concentrate. I try to open my lungs as much as possible, filling them with as much air as I can.

I exhale. I feel my mother's lungs pushing out the carbon dioxide. Mom's inhale is weak, but feels enormous. Now her exhale. Her body is struggling. I feel her life force.

I am in an altered state. I lie still in bed and focus on the exit and return of the life force in her body. My body tries to take her place, imagining every breath she takes, every aspect of her effort. I feel I *am* her, somehow trying to breath for her.

I feel the surge of all the changes in my body. Breathing dominates everything. Her lungs. Her heart. Her thoughts. Lying here, I feel as if I am breaking down each second into one million pieces to try and repair what might be broken. My awareness of my breathing is heightened, I am in contact with every atom filling my lungs.

I can hear her breathe. A constant. Life depends on it. There is a sense of struggle in her breathing.

I am transported into her body, imagining her breathing, gasping, taking in as much oxygen as I can to fill her body for her survival. Does she need help? Why do I feel this way? I remain in bed, actively involved in every breath I take. My focus is on her breath, her body.

Can the energy of the universe transport me into her? We are in union breathing, and I feel this. The effort is not natural. I am searching for a balance to ease the struggle. Does she need help?

"Shushana, are you okay?"

It's Jack. "Come outside," he says, "and watch the sunset. It's beautiful." I notice in the corner of my eye that it's about eight o'clock.

"No, Jack," I say, "you go outside and enjoy." I can tell he is worried about me by the way he hesitates in the doorway, but he leaves, and I remain in bed and focus on breathing, breathing as a machine would do, so as to not cause any skip in the breath. I stay in bed for several more hours, concentrating on her breathing and organs.

Later I rise and realize it is way too late to call her. She will be asleep. I eventually sleep, too.

Brrring. It's the phone. Six in the morning. My brother Steve gets right to the point. "We took Mom to the emergency urgent care," he says. "She is in the hospital. She is having a hard time breathing."

Jack and I take a plane to Houston that evening.

I did not realize last night that these were some of her final breaths. How could I have known? Eleven days later, she breaths no more.

Ivory and Olive

We are told this will be her last night with us. I'm sitting in the intensive care unit on the hospital bed beside my mother, staring at her face. Even near death, she is beautiful. It's all so hard to comprehend. I was speaking with my mother as she sat in a chair just an hour ago, and now they say in a few hours she will be gone. Why didn't they know this before?

I do not take my eyes off my mother. Leaning on her bed are her children and grandchildren. We take turns holding her hands. Her lips loudly speak every word of the Our Father as we pray together. She looks me straight in the eyes to make sure I am saying it, too. Her voice is strong, not skipping a beat. She'll be gone in a few hours? I'm still in disbelief.

Mom is no stranger to this floor. She volunteered for decades here at St. Luke's Hospital and spent over ten thousand volunteer hours at the heart institute and in the ICU talking to patients and families, interpreting languages for them. She worked side by side with the world-renowned surgeons of the Texas Medical Center, and now we are here in the department of the doctor she most admired and enjoyed working with, heart surgeon Dr. Denton Cooley.

Shortly after the prayer, she seems to be sleeping, perhaps no longer aware of us in her presence. I have seen many people pass in my life. I realize there is less blood circulation, fewer heart beats and less air. Our physical bodies change. But I've never seen anything like what I'm observing now. I stare at her deeply, aware of every second that goes by.

Her face is gorgeous—rested and calm—her breath is slow and quiet. Her skin, as always, is flawless with a natural glow. People have always complimented her on her gorgeous complexion, ivory with a hint of olive. And as I watch, something begins to happen—the very tiny lines around her eyes and chin completely disappear, as if someone skilled in Photoshop is erasing the lines to tight perfection. Her face is transforming—it's as if she's becoming younger. It happens quickly.

Intently, I stare at her. What is happening? Her skin appears so youthful and healthy, radiating peak beauty.

Now, just before she dies, there's no sign of even one very tiny line, only the most beautiful porcelain face I have ever seen in my entire life. Her face is perfect. She is here dying, and I see heaven. Her inner beauty and soul take over the outside. I feel God and the universe saying something to me—offering me a glimpse of God.

It's so big for me, watching this, a miracle before my eyes, a most holy moment. I stare at her immaculate skin. Godly, I think. Her expression is serene. I am mystified, overtaken by her transformation. I know it was meant for me to witness.

Only later do I consider that although her body was dying, she was being prepared for a different life, for whatever comes next. Her skin became like a newborn's, pure and perfect. Even as she died, she became new. God blessed me as a witness to her new birth.

How do I describe that I saw God's hand showing heaven in her face?

Gravediggers

"I loved sitting on her lap," Vincent says to me. "All her hugs." We're reminiscing about Mom, my cousin and I. He called her "My Mommie Mary." He loved her so much. Her funeral's only a couple days away, and I love the way his stories honor her. They return me to Los Angeles, where I was born. I remember the apple tree in front of the house that I climbed when I was four. Though he was five years older than I, Vincent and I often played in the yard there together, and Mom loved showering him with her sincere attention.

But this morning, I'm having a hard time focusing on Vincent's stories—my mind keeps returning to yesterday's conversation with the gravesite manager. He said they'd be digging the hole for Mom's grave this afternoon.

A seed of a thought has been growing since he said that. I want to care for her ground. I want to participate in her gravesite preparation. Shouldn't it be the family who uncovers the earth and prepares the land to receive a loved one? Her resting place is next to my father,

9

sacred ground. The urge becomes increasingly pressing. I check my watch. Almost nine thirty. I want to fill my hands with the dirt where she will lay. I want to feel her new earth. It will help comfort me, help ease the pain of her loss, help reconcile the earth's new gain.

"And then there was the time . . .," says Vincent, launching into another "My Mommie Mary" story.

"Vincent," I say, making a move to leave, "I have some business to take care of."

"What is it?" he says.

"I really need to be involved with my mother's grave," I say, "and I want to put the shovel into the dirt and have the first dig, at minimum. They are scheduled to dig her grave this afternoon. I want to go. Now."

He looks surprised at my choice of action, but his eyes fill with enthusiasm. "Can I go?" he asks.

"Sure," I say. I tell him where to get the shovels in the shed behind the house, and within a minute, we are in my car and on our way.

It takes twenty minutes to arrive at the cemetery gates, then we drive the beautiful, winding roads through the decorated monuments and gravestones. As I descend a hill at ten miles an hour, we see a tractor in the distance at her grave. Its fork and huge teeth are about four feet away from the earth where she will lay.

The man sitting in the driver's seat is moving the controls to change the direction of the teeth to dig into the earth in the precise location of her new home. I race the car up to the spot, honking the horn.

"Stop!" I scream, and though the car is still in motion, Vincent and I both open our car doors to leap out. "Stop! Stop!" Vincent is waving his hands to get the driver's attention. Later, he would say to me, "There wasn't even anywhere near one minute to spare before the tractor teeth were going to shove into the dirt." We both knew the ground breaking was literally seconds away.

"Please," I say to the driver and his work partner, "please move away."

The men give us a look of confusion. They have a job to do.

"*Basta, basta*," I say in Spanish. They understand my attempts. They hesitate, but understand my needs. The driver slips off the tractor and walks a short distance away with the other man.

Vincent and I bring our shovels from the car and begin to dig. The gravediggers watch us for five minutes, then walk further away, giving us privacy. We first dig into the grass. Our shovels slice right in. We put the dirt aside. The dirt is heavy for me. Twisting the shovel to spill the dirt onto the ground is putting pressure on my injured wrist, but this task feels more important than anything else in my life. The soil feeds us, and from it, we will continue.

Touching the earth and sweating over her grave feels good. In my sadness, I feel energy soaring. I am still caring for her, as I did in the hospital, as she did for me all my life. It might be the last direct attention I can give her body. This is where her body—in the beautiful white casket with the bluebirds decorating the sides—will live.

Vincent and I work two areas of the site. We are silent and focused. We dig and put the earth aside, dig and put the earth aside. This preparation satisfies my sense of duty. Our feet press hard on the shovels to push them as deep down as they will go. I feel I am giving Mom my love from my hands; my dripping sweat will remain with her. We dig for almost an hour. It becomes difficult when we both begin hitting thick, live, rope-like roots. Then we get stuck with a root the size of a watermelon. Though we're frustrated, it's clear we have to stop.

Staring at the roots, I think of Mom's advice about family and staying connected: Dream, explore and soar in life above the clouds, beyond the stars, but remain rooted to the ground. Mom talked about *these* roots. There is an excitement in me. I am connecting to my mother's roots. Here she is, reminding Vincent and me to stay close, connected, rooted to love, to our family. Vincent has a look of satisfaction on his face.

We turn the project over to the gravediggers. There are no tears. The work with her dirt is nourishing, transforming—bringing it up and putting it aside. What a gift. It is a blessing.

The men return, one sits on the tractor and controls the fork. The two have such a difficult time breaking up the roots that they need to return with a larger tractor and a huge chain saw. These roots are *solid*.

This was Mom's story. She often spoke of her ancestors and shared their stories as they were passed to her. It seems appropriate that with a beautiful tree right next to her gravesite, there are deep, strong roots.

I enjoy watching the men struggling with Mom's roots—dense and robust. She will eventually come to know these roots in her new earth. I see the two strangers sweat profusely, and drop after drop after drop meets my mother's earth. They are working so hard.

Watching them, I marvel at the timing of our arrival. It was nothing but perfect. In a few seconds, a stranger would have taken my place in preparing this space. The machinery would have cut through the earth in no time. The grave manager had been certain the excavation would happen only in the afternoon, and this morning, we received our blessing. Where did it come from, that urgency to leave the house right away?

Then, a thought drives me to run! Mom always loved to tip the workers that deserve more attention. The person washing dishes. Someone mopping the floors. I run to my car. It feels so good. Joy streams through every nerve in my body. The elation has me almost crying. I can carry out Mom's will.

I had placed Mom's wallet in my purse, wanting it to be near me. Now I am digging again, but this time through my purse. Before I find her wallet, I come across her blue rosary that was on her chest when she passed away. I hold it and feel connected to her life. Then I pull out her wallet and open it up for the big bucks. I take out the money to tip her gravediggers. I can imagine her telling me to give it all to them, this is the last tip she will give.

She touched these bills with her fingers. From her hands to the hands of her gravediggers. They created her new house for her physical body. They are the builders. Mom's builders. Sweating over her home. Sculpting her resting place. I return to the site and offer her gratitude to the gravediggers the way she would have wanted. In her style.

Epilogue

As I write this miracle on my laptop, I am between my mother and father at the cemetery. The birds are singing. I have shade from the tree with the big roots on this hot summer day. The wind is blowing. I feel nourished by their presence. I feel their calm. It converts into my energy. It is comforting.

Ringing Messages

"Why is my phone ringing church bells?"

I can hear Jack's curiosity. I've called him at work. Although my husband has been by my side the last two days since Mom died, I needed to ask him an important question, so I called.

"I'm in a staff meeting," he says. I hear him chuckling as he repeats himself, "and we're all here listening to church bells when you called. Why did you change my phone ring to church bells? You need to change it back."

"Jack, honey, I did not touch your phone," I say. I can tell he doesn't believe me. "I did not take your phone, go to my name, go to ring tones specifically for my name, find the church bells from hundreds of ring sounds, and then change it."

"If you didn't do it," he says, his volume rising, "then one of the boys did it!"

"No," I reply firmly. "None of the boys changed your ring tone. First, they are adults and don't play pranks on you. And second, changing a ringtone to church bells is not considered a prank. Also,

15

why would they even bother to change the ringtone for when I call you to church bells? Plus, they have not even been around you the last couple of days."

After we hang up, I, too, am questioning how Jack's ring for my phone calls has changed to church bells. Of the hundreds of sound choices, how did it change to this? Church bells. So odd. Who changed it?

Mom? Mom *loved* that sound. She felt that the familiar tones were feeding the listener music laced with Godly messages. When the bells rang, she would become quiet and make the sign of the cross. So, is this her? Still inviting us to hear the message of the bells, even though she is not here? But why would she change *Jack's* phone?

Well ... Mom prayed all her life that I would be with a kind, caring, loving, spiritual and loyal partner. Jack is *always* this man. She loved him completely, and she said to me all the time, both in front of him and on the phone, "Treat him well and care for him. What a decent, caring man God blessed you with. Always respect him, because he is an angel. You have an angel in your life."

That's it. The church bells are Mom pointing at my love, Jack, pointing to say what a blessing he is, asking me to fully appreciate and take care always of my angel.

In reflection, the church bells gave me another message from her. "There is a purpose in the bells," Mom would say, "a meaning beyond the sound." I can hear her say, "Shushana, think about going to church! Pray and always behave kindly!" In a few days, I will be going to church for her funeral. It will be my first visit in a very long time.

Is this Mom projecting a new reality for me? Telling me to grow in my relationship with God?

Once I lean into her message, I find it very comforting. What a gift. Mom is using her love for church bells to give me a push in the right direction—just when I need it the most.

Epilogue

Jack still keeps the church bells ringing on his cell phone.

Thorns

I sat in Mom's chair in the vanity area in her bathroom. Though she'd passed away two days ago, I could still feel her energy and presence, her breath still here. I thought of Mom resting on this chair every day since I was a teenager, how she'd think of her day ahead, how this space contains almost a lifetime of daily reflection—all her hopes for her day, her prayers.

I thought of her reflection in the mirror—her thick hair with its natural curl and shine, her glowing silky ivory skin with a hint of olive color, her high cheek bones that accentuated her long almond-shaped dark brown eyes.

We had so much fun here together. Mom loved it when I brushed her hair. I'd help her get dressed, watch her put on her perfume, and help her prepare for her volunteer work, parties, dinners at the house and for everyday life.

She took very little time to get ready. Often, with her, I'd try to get her to wear more makeup, but she would respond, "Sweetheart I am beautiful the way I am now." Then she'd shower me with her big, sincere smile.

Her lipsticks filled a container on her vanity. I picked up one realizing her lips touched inside this tube. Her lips were on every lipstick here, her lips pressed onto the colors in every tube. I opened one and stared at it, thinking of her. I said a prayer, and I kissed her lips. The lipstick touched my lips and I kissed my mother. Though it helped me feel closer to her, I was heartbroken, grieving.

The mirrored counter was covered in beautiful porcelain ornaments we purchased together over the years, including four colorful hand-painted angel statues. I remembered when we bought the small, ornate French tray with picturesque scenes painted on it. The matching bottles were there on top. My eyes were exploring the area, then stopped at two Clinique lotion bottles. I became fixated on them. My heart dropped. I felt sick to my stomach. I stared at them, feeling totally worthless. A feeling of anger took over. I felt like a nobody. Without purpose. Useless.

They were turned upside down for Mom to get the last drops. There was nothing in them at all.

About two months earlier she'd asked me, "Please can you just get me a Clinique lotion bottle, I am running out of lotion." She only used Clinique on her face. "I need some," she'd said. She put her soothing lotion on her face every day. That was the extent of her morning face ritual. A little Clinique, and she felt polished.

I had completely forgotten this one simple request so important for her daily ritual. I felt worthless. Mom rarely asked me to do anything for her, and what a pleasure it was when she did. My heart felt dull and paralyzed. She just died. I cannot tell her, "Oops, I forgot, Mom." I can't ask her, "Why didn't you say something again to me?"

I wanted to cry. I have time for myself, time for my husband and family, my dog, my friends. But I failed to get her lotion, and she never brought it up again. She did not want to bother me. She'd asked, and I had not delivered.

The upside-down bottles told me she tried to get out to any last possible tiny drop. The clear glass sides of the bottles were devoid of any lotion. They'd been empty for a long time, I could tell.

Forgetting her simple need put me at a very low point. Love is about meeting one another in times of need, especially when we are asked. Getting lotion is as easy as a click on the laptop to order. I felt ashamed, not at all the daughter I wanted to be.

A few days later, I am back at my house in my own vanity, where I prepare myself each morning. This morning I dress myself for her final time above earth, her funeral day. The ache is so painful, my heart so heavy. Mom always believed in her eternal future with God, however, I am coming to terms with the fact that her hugs and kisses are now only a memory.

I stare at my face in the mirror and prepare to put on my lotion. I, too, am down to the last drop. Days earlier, I had taken the pump straw out of the bottle and rubbed my fingers up and down it to take off any lotion on the straw, but because the lotion is extremely light and thin, virtually none stays on the straw. The sides and bottom are already rubbed clean from my cotton swab scraping them to get the last remaining lotion.

As I scraped the bottle every morning for the last few days, I was reminded of my mother's struggle to get lotion from her bottles and it refueled my guilt.

Frustrated, I unscrew the pump and pull out the straw to place it on the counter so I can swab any last remaining lotion.

What is this? I stare at the plastic straw. Every nerve in my body seizes. I turn the plastic straw to look at all of it. It's less than two inches long, and it's loaded with lotion in the shapes of rose thorns, four of them. Thick, big, prominent, soft and moist thorns. They are the *exact* shape and size of large rose thorns, with a dot of lotion at the end where they curl up and slightly tuck in.

They look like sculptures of rose thorns, in cream. They dominate the straw. I stare into the tiny bottle, certain these thorns of lotion were not covering my little straw in the bottle the day before and before and before. How can the straw come up with four big rose thorns? Now, I am not seeing lotion, but thorns. Revelation. Mom.

Mom often said, "In life you have the thorns with beauty." It was her guiding metaphor, teaching us to address and to deal with any difficult situation with compassion and understanding, to circle all life with love. And here is Mom's voice coming to me in rose thorns, her love and wisdom echoing in many forms.

A miracle changes the moment. I stop ravaging myself with guilt. Calmness and peace fill me. I do not doubt what my eyes see. My mother is here. Spirit is formless. Without dimension. This *is* happening. The truth flows from a spectrum that cannot be extinguished.

Preparing for Mom's funeral, I rub my fingers along all the thorns of lotion from the straw. There is more than enough. My face is supple and moist. I prepare myself to stand at the altar and speak about my mother.

I don't feel like a useless daughter any longer. She understands. She is present and all aware. Eternity is not so distant. Eternity is now.

I understand, Mom. I get it. Let this go. You are fine. I am fine.

Epilogue One

The following week, I gave into my science side. I needed to experiment with this lotion to make sense of what happened.

I purchased a new bottle and removed the pump from the bottle. No lotion sticking out in any shape from the straw. It held almost no lotion on it. The lotion was so thin, it barely covered the plastic. You could see the plastic rather than lotion. I shook the bottle to try and get it to make the rose thorns shapes sticking out and curling up. Nothing. Not any shape could be created even from a full bottle. Though my brain craved a clear explanation, I stopped tampering with the miracle, stopped doubting it.

Epilogue Two

Miracles of abundance were not unusual in Mom's life. Here's one story she told me.

One night, Mom received a call from a friend, a foreign diplomat. As was her pleasure, Mom invited the friend and her immediate family, about six people, over for dinner the following evening.

The next day, she and Dad made some of Mom's favorite dishes, preparing enough for about ten people. That evening she heard car doors slamming in front and looked out the window to see her guests arrive. Car after car pulled up and parked on the street in front of the house. Doors kept opening, and more and more people were getting out, walking onto the sidewalk and towards the house. Her friend had brought an entourage. Through the window, Mom counted at least twenty people.

Her heart sank. She had food to feed, at most, ten. She felt dizzy and almost passed out. How could she explain she did not prepare food for everyone? It was so out of keeping with her standards for hospitality. She always made three times more food than she thought was needed, but this time, considering the short notice, she'd decided to make only enough. She needed a miracle.

"God," she said, "help me to feed all my guests. Please, do what you did with the fish and bread miracles before. I need this to happen tonight."

The food never stopped. Everyone was very well fed and ate two plates of her delicious food. Then there was more.

I will never forget her voice on the phone, her panic and awe. She believed so emphatically that God intervened and provided for her in her time of desperation.

Epilogue Three

The thorns of lotion story reminds me of the time Mom called asking why I removed the one red rose from the clear vase over her refrigerator. Her voice was very upset, shaky, loud and almost crying. It was very rare to hear her upset like this.

"You know how important the flower is to me," she said. "I told you to never take it out, why did you remove it? Just because it is dry does not mean you make decisions to take it down."

She continued, "Marie Rose [her housekeeper] said she did not touch it, and I believe her. She knows to never remove it. You know how important this flower is to me. You are the only one who would take it out. Why did you? I am so upset!"

I understood the seriousness. This was her sacred rose and it was gone. It would be only me or Maria Rosa who would clean her house and help Mom personally.

I halfway convinced her I did not take the rose, since there was no logic in this event. I would not go on a ladder, climb up stairs to get it from the center of the tall refrigerator and throw it away.

I reminded Mom that I was the one who took her to view the casket of Saint Therese when her body came to Houston over ten years ago. That I was there when the rose that lay on Saint Therese's casket was given to her. That I know it is her treasure. I would never remove it.

"No one took it, Mom," I said. "I saw it the other day, there, standing in its vase, same place it has been since it was placed there."

She paused and thought. Though the sound of worry was still in her voice, she calmed down and spoke softly, "The rose in the vase over the refrigerator is gone."

She repeated the story of the rose, how it lay on the casket of Saint Therese when her body traveled to Houston. How she put her hand on the casket and prayed to Saint Therese, this saint she admired. How the saint herself was called a flower.

Later, Mom told me she realized the disappearance was a message from God. She had made a promise to God that she was not paying attention to, and she believed the missing flower was a reminder to improve upon her promise since she made that promise when she received the rose while at Saint Therese's casket. She said she put her efforts toward her promise and she received an answer from God that she must continue with the map she created in her promise and the path carved for her.

Maybe on Mom's funeral day, the missing rose appeared to me with its soft, supple thorns.

Stairway to Heaven

It's the morning of my mother's funeral. The house is quiet, but my mind is abuzz, thinking of what to share with the hundreds of friends and family members who will be at her service. I've waited until this morning to prepare my words so I can be in the moment with them, and now I'm flooded with all I want to say.

Say, for instance, how easily she created peace in any environment. How she was an educator of love. I want to speak of her generosity. Her joy. And her love for the song "Stairway to Heaven."

"Stairway to Heaven," a hard rock classic by Led Zeppelin, was one of my favorite songs growing up. During high school, I would play it in my room, volume full blast. Whether early morning or late night, Mom practically invited it.

"I love that song so much, the stairway to heaven," she would say. "That beautiful stairway that takes you to heaven. Create your life here filled with kindness, God and love. Shushana, believe and never doubt there is heaven. God is in the song."

It was a joke to me then that she truly thought it was a spiritual song, focusing as she did on the last line of the song when the lead singer gently chants, "and she's buying a stairway to heaven." Mom took it to heart, envisioning heaven in that last line. I think it's the only line she ever paid attention to! But it fit with her firm beliefs—that heaven is our future home—and the "carrying stairways" often entered our conversations.

This morning, I'm debating whether or not to share with everyone my affection for the song and Mom's view of it. Is too superficial of a story? Should I give the time to other stories?

When I walk into the family room, my cousin Vincent is already there.

"Vincent," I say, "Can I run something by you?"

"Of course!" he says.

I tell him I want to include the story about "Stairway to Heaven," how much Mom loved it and how the song has meaning to me.

"Tell the story," he says. "That is what people want to hear, something personal."

Though I haven't heard this song in many, many years, the memory of Mom and me and our conversations about it feels fresh, and I decide to speak about it at the altar.

An hour before Mom's funeral, we walk out to Jack's white SUV. We say nothing as we get in the car. The silence feels right. Jack opens the passenger door for me, then closes it. Vincent and his wife Sue get in the back. Jack turns the key, the engine hums, then quiets. The radio comes on with the car.

I know that note, that first quiet note of solo acoustic guitar. I look at Jack. He does not look at me. In the back, Vincent's eyes widen, full of surprise. He looks stunned.

I turn up the volume all the way. Music floods the car. Jack does not ask me to turn it down. The first note of our song, "Stairway to Heaven," came on the station the second the engine quieted. I feel her. I feel us. She is with all of us.

Vincent remains speechless. We're all mesmerized, listening to the song as we drive to the church. We arrive at the red light across the street from the church just as the song is about to end.

Sitting at the intersection, I see the hearse. Mom's body, I know, is inside it in her white casket. There's a pause in the song as the instruments stop playing, and my eyes focus on the big cross in front of the church. I remember my mother always making the sign of the cross when she drives by this intersection. I am indulging in one of the first miracles after her death. I wait for the last line of the song, staring at her hearse and the cross.

The last line of the song rings in our ears, "And she's buying a stairway to heaven."

I make the sign of the cross.

Growing Curiosity

Her house feels so empty. It's only been a week since Mom's death, and now this house that I lived in most of my life is so still and quiet. The kitchen feels empty. The space in front of her big windows where she loved to relax, empty. The family room, empty. Yet every room is full of memories. She was walking around here just the other day. She was fixing tea and dinner for us all.

Looking out the windows, I see the backyard and patio where she loved to soak up Vitamin D and the sun's energy. Even in hundred-degree weather and at age eighty-one, she enjoyed the radiant heat. Basking there was an everyday ritual. If we did not find her inside the house, all of Mom's grandchildren and family knew to find her on the patio, and all of us had, at some time, sat outside on the patio with her.

Yes, outside is where I need to be now, to feel the sun beaming as she felt it. Perhaps that will slow my thoughts down. Maybe the birds will sing. I will sit in her chair. It will help comfort my shattered heart.

I walk out onto the pale pink bricks of the patio. At times, it is lined with roses. There are four chairs, all of them iron mesh with large holes throughout the iron, and a matching table. Mom always sat in the same chair, facing the view of her grapevines. My father had planted them for her here in Houston as an homage to her Baghdad traditions, and twenty-five years later, they still grow on a trellis that stands next to the patio. There are posts to support the six-foot-tall platform. The top is flat. The vines wind their way up the posts, then cascade down the edges of the top, creating a thick umbrella of leaves and grapes that hang below the trellis.

"Oh, I love my grape leaves. They are so pretty," she would say, giddy as a child, as if it were the first time she saw them. It took little to please Mom, and she must have repeated these phrases a thousand times.

I approach her chair to sit myself, but I am thrown out of my memory and into the present when I notice I cannot sit there. Something is on it. Through it. Growing into it. A grapevine has woven itself through her chair! The chair itself looks so alive! The vine enters a mesh hole and infuses the chair with leaves and buds.

What's astonishing is the path the vine had to take to arrive at her chair. I study the plant. Instead of draping in its usual umbrella pattern, one lone vine has grown upward, making its way onto the rooftop, then growing across the roof about twelve feet before angling down. But then it must have positively defied gravity to grow away from the house at a wide angle to latch onto Mom's chair. The vine easily could have continued to grow all across the roof, but instead it grew away. Logic bending. Thrilling.

The vine put in a lot of effort to reach her chair. Why not the other chairs? Why not the table? Was the grapevine motivated by this chair? Did the chair call to it? Is the growth of this grapevine wildly out of line? Or is it exactly where it wants to be?

The beauty of the vine merging with Mom's chair fills the empty space in the seat where my mom would be, and it fills the empty space in my heart, too, where I ache for her. I do not sit on her chair, so as not to crush the emerging vine. I admire the way it lifts itself upwardly, lifts as Mom's spirit does, in the most unexpected places.

"I want my grape leaves to last forever," Mom had said. "I love them."

Is this her at play in her leaf-wrapped chair? I marvel at how Mom shows her love and her distinct presence in her twisted grapevines, on her porch in the sun. I hear her telling me this is the hand of God that has guided the vines to its unlikely destination.

Happy Birthday, Baby!

"Ooooooooooh. Ahhhhhgg. Ahhhg. Ooooooooo."
It sounded like the woman on the other end of the phone was giving birth. She wasn't. It was my mother.

Every year, two days before my birthday, Mom would call simply to remind me that many years ago she was going into labor at that time. She emphasized her pains and anticipation of giving birth.

Then, the day before my birthday, she would call and repeat herself again, this time adding sounds that would imitate a woman with hard labor pains. Every year she moaned and screamed and we'd laugh together as she re-enacted my birth. These performances were so comical, I saved some of them on my voicemail to share with friends.

But the *real* laugh, without failure, was on my birthday. I was born 8:22 a.m., California time. She'd call me 8:22 a.m. California time *and* 8:22 a.m. Texas time to go through her entire stand-up routine of giving birth to me. She topped it off with her perfected cry of a newborn. Every year I endured this, my mother imitating my first sounds. She couldn't help but laugh at herself. She nailed the newborn cry, and she knew it. Then she'd say in a child's voice, "Little tiny baby girl." And then, she would repeat what her doctor said to her as he held me by one foot upside down, "You have your baby girl." That same doctor, she said, had told her she was definitely having a boy.

Since her death two weeks before, I'd been coming to terms with the fact that she would not be calling me on my birthday and that my last laugh with her and the birthday comedy ended last year. My gut already hurt from its absence. For the last several decades, I'd delighted in her vivacious description of my birth.

Jack and I decided to spend my birthday at our remote home in the wilderness of Colorado. The distance away from Mom's home in Houston made me feel anxious, imbalanced, but I told myself that territory no longer separates me from her. Now, she is spirit. There is no map to measure our distance from each other.

On the morning of my birthday, my sleep is broken by a strange sound. The sound is distinct and clear. Adrenaline runs through my veins. A new born baby crying. It is in my room.

What is going on? I listen to this baby cry. It must be outside my window, though it seems to be coming from inside. I hear a breath, then "Waaaah." It's exactly the sound a newborn baby makes, "Waaaah." And then again, "Waaaah."

There is an open window about ten feet from my head. Could this be an elk or baby deer? No. I've heard baby elk and deer for fourteen years, and this sound is coming from neither. Plus, it's in my room. And it's loud. And it's a human sound, a human baby. Now

I'm wide awake. And spooked, too spooked to get out of bed. I know what I heard. Not an elk. Not a deer. A baby crying, and sounds as if it is in my room!

I look at my cell phone. 7:22 a.m. That is 8:22 a.m. in Texas. Feeling a miracle. I hear Mom. It's the time of my birth when Mom *always* calls me.

Eventually, I walk to the breakfast room and tell our houseguests David and Lynn about the baby cries that I heard. Their bedroom is at the end of the house.

"Yes," says David, "I heard the baby, too, this morning. It was loud, and I didn't know if you maybe had other guests? But I heard it coming from outside."

We talk about what it might have been. David is an outdoorsman, and he, like me, rules out the possibility that it was a baby elk or deer. He stares right at me, his eyes big. "No," he says, "It sounded like a human baby."

What could have made that sound? Thinking of baby cries, I remember. Mom said to me the happiest sound she ever heard in her life was my cry when I was born.

She is here, leaving me her birthday message at her usual clock time, a surprise birthday gift that will last a lifetime. There is no space between us. The door is wide open.

Time and Face

The photos of Mom are lined up next to each other on my bed. One after the other, I hold them up to my face and slowly kiss her lips and cheeks. The gentle touches give me a small reenactment of her last day with us, only three weeks ago.

The emptiness in my gut hurts. How can I see her face again? I cannot imagine the road ahead. I need her face. These photos bring me closer to her loving smile, her dancing eyes, her soft curly hair.

My instinct is to protect the photos, hoping they can somehow replace her wisdom and the many ways she guided me all of my life. Holding these photos of her face both nourishes me and leaves me hollow. I tell myself, This is what happens. Still, I yearn for her. In every photo her eyes are speaking, piercing into my soul. I hear her voice. I pay attention to every detail in every smile in the photos. They duplicate her liveliness.

Mom expressed to me many times that she asked God to intervene so that when she died, she might be with her family surrounding her, praying. Her wish came true, and at the same time, the event blessed me and filled my spirit. Kissing and caressing her face that day she died was an incredible experience.

Those moments before she passed, she appeared as the most beautiful angel in heaven. Her face was so serene, it was almost tranquilizing. Her skin was glowing and flawless. I was captivated by her physical beauty. Her face spoke a thousand languages of eternal love. That was almost three weeks ago. It seems like yesterday, and it seems like many years ago. I am lost in time.

Her face—her familiar face. I press it close to mine. This is paper, however, her image.

And now it's time to leave for our hike. After Mom's funeral, Jack had recommended we come to Colorado since the wilderness gives me such bliss and centers me. We call this place God's paradise. Nature here is intensely wild and rich. And as much as I want to talk myself out of going on the hike, I know I need it, even if just for pure exercise. Mom would tell me to go, enjoy!

I carefully place the photos on my bedroom counter as if to protect her. Before I leave, I am already anxious to return to her face and to restore my memories. But Jack's right. The wilderness will help me regain some strength and bring me closer to her spirit. This hike will sooth my soul, perhaps provide an escape from my new reality.

And the day is glorious for a hike. The air is calm, the greens are lush. But the hike itself is just a motion. Each step I take, I imagine the song in her eyes looking into mine. I imagine her lips moving with words for me. Her smell. Her kiss. My steps are a little behind Jack's and our friends'. I am mostly quiet, consumed with thoughts of Mom. Her soul radiating with love. Her words playing in my head. She was always available for me, and now every room will have an empty chair.

The mountain path steepens, and my breathing intensifies. I emerge from my thoughts and notice the grass is tall, the sky clear. It's a cool day and the air is light. And then I am back to my thoughts, letting my legs carry me. I see her face, lit up. Mom smiled every time we looked at each other. That would be a million times. She always smiled. Her eyes poured love to us. Her lips spoke kind words. Her hands waved hello and goodbye. Her arms gave big hugs. Kisses were tossed into the air every time I drove away, and, as she watched me leave, I'd see her lips move as she'd say a prayer for my safety. Though I can envision her perfectly, there will be no new pictures.

I make my way up the mountain, stilling lagging behind the group, and my phone makes an odd sound, a beep I've never heard before. I unzip the pocket where I've been carrying it since we started hiking a couple of hours ago, and I pull it out. The mountain is steep, so I stop moving to look at the screen.

On the front of my phone it reads, "**! FaceTime Failed**, Mom is not available for FaceTime." What am I reading? How did this get here? I have never FaceTimed Mom, nor have I ever seen this before. Plus my phone has been on lock. And it is still in lock position. I did not touch my phone. How could these words appear on the front of my phone? In bold, no less, and taking up two lines.

I stop my husband and friends to show them the words that have appeared on my screen. Also astonished, they take a photo of it. My eyes still don't believe what they see.

My heart begins to make sense of it, though. My morning with the photos was a revival, an attempt to bring my mom from the past into my present, a yearning to recapture her face next to mine. And now my phone, out of nowhere—or everywhere—is telling me. "**! FaceTime Failed**, Mom is not available for FaceTime."

Perhaps this is Mom saying, "I am here. I am different, but here, now with you. However, no face time. Be fine with this. You are well."

This has never appeared again.

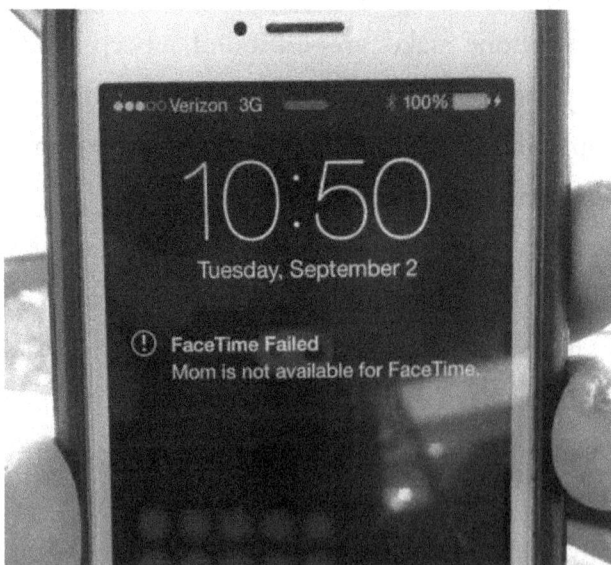

Bringing the
Image to Life

When I was about thirty, my mother gave me a big stack of old black-and-white photos to look at. Most were of her and family. One captured my attention. It was small, three by three inches. Mom appeared so relaxed, happy, sweet and confident. She was lounging on the grass, picnic style, but without a blanket. Her hair was very shiny and coiffed back. Her eyes exuded happiness and softness, and also strength. Between her teeth she held a flower. I didn't know the variety, but it appeared a bit aged or droopy.

I took the photo with me to my house and kept it in a top drawer of my table in my study. When I opened my desk drawer, the photo was in my sight. It roused a very strong connection to Mom. I would even think, Mom is just a phone call away. I see her all the time, though, so it seemed strange that this small black-and-white photo could create the strongest emotions of love and yearning in me.

When I stared into this photo, no matter my mood, it generated a sense of love from her and for her. How could this happen from just a photo? Especially when I was able to get in the car and have lunch with her anytime? I would stare into the photo and experience her entire existence, even if I were seeing her for dinner the same day. The sensation was beyond anything I could explain, an intensity that filled every cell in my body.

I took this tiny photo to a custom photography store and had them enlarge it to an eleven by fourteen. I asked for the flower and her lips to be tinted a hint of red, selected a gorgeous wood frame and hung the image in my study.

It was years later that my mother was in my study and took notice of this photo. She laughed with surprise and joy. She hadn't seen that photo in years and said she remembered that day clearly. She was about five months pregnant with me, her first born.

Until that day in my study, she didn't know this photo filled me with an awakening that caused my soul to soar. And until that day, I didn't know that I was in the photo, too. The two of us as one.

Now, a couple months after she passed away, I find myself in my bathroom brushing my teeth when something inside me tells me to look outside the bathroom window. The pulling is like a chain around my waist, it's so strong. I sense that there is something to be discovered. I have a meeting and must be on time, however I cannot ignore this tug. There is no battle of wills. I follow the tug. These days, the sense of a schedule or time feels irrelevant. My mother's death has allowed me to open my channels for a more spiritual exploration and dedication.

Still brushing my teeth, I crawl over the bathtub rim and walk into the wide tub to look outside the window. I look to the far right, and something catches my eye. I strain to find it. What is it?

As if moved by this magnet force, I walk into the bedroom through a door that leads out to the courtyard. I walk all the way to the end of the courtyard, not knowing what I am looking for, and there I see among all the bushes one white flower.

There it is—blooming out of its season, covered by branches and bright green leaves. There are no buds and no other flowers growing on any of the other bushes that line the house on both sides all the way to the fence. This is my mother's most favorite flower. The gardenia. I would pick gardenias for her every year and take them to her house. It reminded Mom of her childhood.

I put it in a vase on the dining room table, and this one flower showers its scent throughout our home, its sweetness travels even to the back rooms.

The next day, the flower turns a coral red color and shrivels as flowers do when they start to dry. This coral red color is odd. I have had gardenias for years, and I've never seen this in a gardenia before. I place the flower on my desk in my study—it's so unique with its bright color. This flower calls me.

Then I take notice. There it is. A connection to the photo of Mom that I treasure, the one with the flower between her teeth. I lay the 11" x 14" portrait of her flat down on my desk. I look at both flowers. They are identical in shape, size and color. I place the flower from my garden right on top of the flower between her teeth in the photo.

Twin flowers. I can't tell the difference between the photo with or without the flower resting on top. A perfect match. This flower that called me is my new relationship with my mother in this photo. The flower before I was born and now the flower after her death are one. She is here. Her voice enters my quiet awareness. This unification of the two flowers explains my mysterious devotion to this photo. It is more than a photo, it's a story, perhaps a miracle prepared for me before I was born. Now after her death, the story is told. She speaks it to me now.

Forever is now. It was planned all along for the flower to appear in the garden. The evidence brings me peace and calm, and I lean into the enormity of the story.

My heart does not ache. I feel the flow of her melody in my blood. God is talking. She appears before me and shows me how miracles have no boundaries for time, space or shape. They are invitations to fully embrace a greater awareness in us.

Epilogue

Later that day, I was going through letters. I found a note in a birthday card she wrote to me saying, "I have loved you before you were ever born, I have loved you always, I will always love you forever, after I die and in all eternity."

Stop!

What was wrong with her car? Susan had been driving the eight blocks from her home to a friend's house for dinner when her car stopped. It's a road she drives sometimes three times a day, but this time her car came to an abrupt stop.

"It was as if my car was taken over," she told me. "And then it just stopped. I don't recall taking my foot off the accelerator nor putting on the brake. My car would not go. I was on the wrong side of the road and I did not know what happened."

Susan is the mother of the first four children with my brother, Steve. Mom considered her a daughter. Susan lived only four blocks away from "Nana's" house so that the grandkids could run back and forth between houses. And Susan was often at Mom's house, too, to chat with my father about the stock market or to pick up food from Mom. She's is a successful lawyer and a Stanford graduate—a practical, strong-minded woman who knows how to get things done. So, it was especially strange for her to feel as if something else was in charge of her driving.

"Why am I stopped?" she'd asked herself. When she looked to see where she was stopped, she realized she was in front of Nana's house.

"Hi Nana," she'd said. "What do you need? Do you need me? Tell me."

Mom had passed away several months earlier, but Susan told me, "I knew right away Nana had something for me when my car stopped in front of her house." And for the next five to ten minutes, she'd sat there in her car and received a message from Mom.

"She told me to sell my house. To move into Nana's house, to buy my mother's house in San Diego. To raise my last child in Nana's house. Then to buy the business that I wanted. It was basically laid out for me."

Susan continued, "The message itself was crystal clear, a step-by-step plan. It was as if I had thought of this all of my life and knew this was the plan I would follow. It changed my life right there."

In some ways, the plan made little sense. Susan was living in a big, beautiful brand-new house. Mom's house is smaller and was built in the 1950s. "But, Shushana," Susan told me, "though I had never thought of it before, I could have my children at that house. It is a blessed house. Living in her home will be a blessing for us."

While she was still there in the car in front of Nana's house, she'd called my brother Steve. "If you and Shushana are not going to sell the house or rent it," she said, "then I want to live in that house."

Steve had emailed me. "You decide," he wrote. "What do you want, sister?"

The event was not only a miracle for Susan, it was a blessing to me. I had been really struggling, not knowing what was going to happen to my mother's house after her death. Mom herself had said, "I hope the house stays just the way it is. I want this house filled with love."

The thought of Susan living in Mom's house with the grandkids coming and going fulfilled my mother's wishes and mine, too. Susan said this plan never crossed her mind, nor had it mine. Mom had orchestrated the perfect plan. Susan had contacted her Realtor right away to sell her home.

When I asked her if moving into Mom's house gave her something she did not have before, she told me, "It's like living in a big hug all the time—extremely blessed. The people that come in are blessed. I feel safe. I raise my children with hugs and blessings."

Epilogue

It was just over three years (in fact 1,122 days) after Mom died that I called Susan to interview her about this miracle. Thirty minutes before our scheduled interview time at one thirty, Susan was rummaging through her safety deposit box to find a car insurance title. She saw a sealed envelope with the word "Nana" on it. Nana had given it to her seven years before, in 2010, and told her to open it in case of emergency. She had completely forgotten about it. It was a full-page letter in Mom's handwriting to Susan. In the letter, Mom gave clear instructions that if anything should happen to me or Steve, her house was for Susan and the children. Though Mom had never mentioned it to any of us, Susan moving into her home had been part of Mom's vision all along.

Not My Hands

How can I forget something so important? Mom had shown me several times the location of the keys to her large steel cabinets—they were in the pocket of an old jacket she did not wear. She'd kept the keys in the same place for decades.

This evening I need to get into the cabinets to access important papers, but the keys are nowhere to be found. I've been cleaning out her house for months since her death. It's a blessing, to be with all her belongings. I can feel her presence here. Her clothes smell of her perfume. But right now, I'm emotionally wiped out and physically drained of all energy. My brain cannot function. And I am at a loss.

I already went through her clothes months ago and did not find the keys. I'd saved only the clothes with fond memories. Any clothes I'd given away, I'd searched every pocket first. Maybe I was sloppy? Perhaps I should check again in the pockets of the clothes I've saved, but I am too so exhausted. I can't even draw up enough energy to walk to the other closet and start going through clothes. But I need to access those personal valuables under lock.

I lean my shoulders against the steel cabinets. They're cold. It does not matter. I could fall asleep standing up. Where are the keys? Which of her jackets was it?

I feel so incompetent. Mom would be anxious knowing I do not have the keys. She might think I was not paying attention to her, that I do not value her instructions. What a brain dead person I am. I feel so small. I am angry with myself and very tired. The lock cannot be picked open. I'll need to schedule a locksmith.

Leaning against the cold steel, a strong force like a magnet pulls me away from the cabinets. Without thought or hesitation I am in a corner staring at a shelf four foot deep that is stacked with at least thirty small boxes, two large boxes, a jewelry box, decorated boxes, a bag of ribbons and a stack of purses over two feet high. I look up and down at all the stuff on the shelves.

I worry that I am wasting time. I need to look for the keys. Yet the pull has drawn me here with no apparent goal. I don't know what I am doing, no idea what I am looking for or what might happen.

My hands mechanically reach into the middle of the stack of purses—not into the attractive thirty-plus gift boxes that I admired, nor the beautiful large jewelry box. One hand holds the stack of purses so they will not fall as the other pulls on an unseen purse in the middle. Out comes a small brown purse with a top zipper. These are not my hands moving. I have become alert to this force.

I aggressively dig into this almost empty purse, not understanding why I am doing this. Tissues are everywhere. Lots and lots of tissue inside. I pull out a couple of business cards. Then, compelled, I open the small side zipper only to find more tissues. I pull them all out. I decide to unravel them also, not understanding. Why am I doing this? And there, heavily wrapped inside many tissues, are two little steel keys. Staring at them, I know immediately these keys will open the cabinet. *And* I know Mom *never* told me the keys were here. This force had purpose.

Grateful and astonished, I slip the key into the lock, and the cabinet opens. Thank you, God. Thank you, Mom.

Setting the Timer

I am imagining it—a massive platter piled high with dolma—stuffed grape leaves, stuffed onions, stuffed zucchini, stuffed tomatoes, stuffed bell peppers—and other platters equally delicious. Every inch of the long table is covered with food. The air smells of spice. The chairs around the dining room table are filled with the world's best doctors, world leaders and family all relaxing and laughing and bantering. And Mom, standing in the kitchen doorway, smiles and urges people to eat.

The memories around this table are priceless. Thousands of interesting conversations. Cooking and hosting parties gave Mom tremendous pleasure. She loved when people gathered in this room to enjoy her food.

And now it is several months since her death. The house is quiet and I am alone, tidying up. Most of the rooms have been organized, her most precious belongings placed in boxes. Today I approach the dining room. I set my phone on the table. It feels empty. Still, it is beautiful—a hand-painted Italian table, brown on the top and pale yellow, cream and gold on the sides. It was designed for eight people, but Mom liked to cram ten and more. It would be tight, but no one minded the closeness.

I find an oversized blue and white photo album tucked away on a bottom shelf of her cabinet. It seems old, but in excellent condition. I lean against a wood cabinet on the floor and begin flipping through pages of photos. Some are photos I took thirty years ago of Mom right in this place. Her smile is wide and her eyes, singing. I smile back at her.

I flip another page but my joy disappears. She is not here. An instant sadness fills me, knowing there will never be another time with her. I will not watch her excitement to feed family and friends. Her famous meals cannot be duplicated; however, the talk of her food can last forever.

Half an hour later, I am still sitting on the same spot on the floor, approaching the last few pages of the photo album when my phone starts to ring and ring and ring. It's a familiar sound, but it's not my normal ringtone. I've never heard this sound on my phone before. It's a very loud, fast succession of rings, one ring after another.

I walk around the table to my phone and stare at it in its lock position. I pick it up. There's no one there. Yes, I think. There is. Mom.

This ringing is the same sound as her old food timer she used over and over when making her feasts. I remember how it would repetitively ring over and over from the kitchen, loud, like an old phone from the 1950s. This ringing was the exact same tone, quick and fast.

Mom has communicated with me by phone several times since her death, enough that I know this is no coincidence, no one-in-a-million chance. This is a message, a delivery from the dimensionless place where she is existing, a reminder that she is with me, aware of my appreciation for the thousands of meals she prepared with her loving hands and the special times she created for everyone who gathered in this one room.

Though I cannot explain it, somehow she knows what is happening to me right now. She has a view, a window to our lives. I am forever grateful.

She Still Has a
Hand in the Dough

"**I** really wish you had learned to make *kulecha*," my niece Caroline says to me. And she's not the only one who's thinking that.

"Yeah," says her brother Tommy. "Why didn't you?" They are both looking at me with puzzled expressions, wondering why I didn't learn to make my mother's famous cookies, beautiful yeast-dough spirals with decorated edges. "You'll score it, Auntie," says their sister Laura. "Go for it"!

Since Mom has passed away, I've heard from them many times how much they miss Nana's cookies. "Nana's were the best," they say, "with just the right amount of sugar," says Caroline. "And the walnuts ground just the right size," says Tommy. And my brother adds, "I love that texture. Nobody can get that great texture the way Nana did. And the smell! God! There were so good!"

I can see on their faces the kids are disappointed I don't know how to make Nana's cookies *exactly* as she makes them.

"Okay!" I say. "I will reproduce Nana's cookies!"

Their cheers erupt, reminding me of a football game touchdown, and their elation propels me into action.

Problem is, not only do I not know how to make *her* kulecha, I don't know how to make kulecha *at all*. I've never even made dough. Though I love to cook, I do not bake bread, and I've never made cookies. I'm a stovetop cooker. I use the oven for vegetables.

I remember Mom used yeast, but I know nothing about yeast. She would add it to the bowl and make the sign of the cross into the dough, praying for the dough to rise for the next day. I am clueless how it works. Right now, I need that cross to help me with this attempt.

Since there's no recipe from Mom, I'll have to punt. I'm sure I need flour, but what kind? Whenever I walk down the baking aisle, I'm struck by how many kinds of flour there are. Wow, I think, this is going to be an ordeal. And since Jack and I are leaving for Colorado in two days, tomorrow night is the only time I will have to make them.

When tomorrow night comes, I am exhausted. Fatigue hits me like a train. I don't think I've slept for thirty-six hours. I get like this with major project deadlines for work.

Although I am wiped out, I am determined to surprise my family with my attempt at making Nana's divine cookies. And the cookie project isn't just for them—I need to follow through for my own self-good.

"I've never seen you so tired," Jack says. "How about I drive you to the grocers?" Though it's only three blocks away, I take him up on his offer.

We walk together to the yeast section, but they are sold out. How can they run out of yeast in such a big grocery store? The manager checks the back inventory and returns, empty handed. I must look really disappointed, because he suggests I ask the store's bakery if they will give me yeast. "Tell them the store is out of stock," he says. I do as he suggests.

"No, ma'am," says the man behind the counter. "I'm sorry, but we cannot be liable."

By now, it is ten at night, and the thought of going to another store makes me even more tired. "Let's go home, Jack," I say. "I'm too drained and deliriously tired. I need to sleep." And that is what we do.

Early the next morning, I go into the kitchen, open the refrigerator and look through the shelves, thinking about what to make for breakfast. And I'm stunned. Here, in the upper top right, on the front of the shelf with its label on the jar facing me, is a jar of yeast. I reach for it, not understanding in any way how or why the jar is here. It has already been opened and is outdated by a year. It's well past its expiration. I do not use yeast, and I have never purchased yeast. And yet it is here in front. How?

Yeast in my fridge? And expired? By now, my housekeeper would have thrown this out. And in a glass jar? A glass jar would not be in the front at the top shelf. Small glass jars go in the arm of the refrigerator. My housekeeper is a perfectionist. She is always on top of cleaning our refrigerator and pantry, discarding outdated items at least once a week. She keeps everything fresh and very well organized in the fridge.

I hold the jar for a very long time, witnessing the impossible, almost feeling my mother's hands around it. What if, somehow, she is behind this event? Or in front of it? Are miracles disguised just like this, in ways for us to think and ponder the miracle? Can we open our minds to infinite possibilities?

Epilogue

Mom would make batches of kulecha twice a year—once around Thanksgiving, just a few days from my brother's birthday, and another batch in the summertime. She'd bake hundreds of them, freezing some so that they could last for a couple of months so that she'd have some for when the kids and close friends came over.

After she died, I was cleaning out her freezer and my niece Samantha came over. I found frozen kulecha, with a note from Mom. On the paper, she'd drawn a heart, and inside it, she'd written, "For my dear, sweet Samantha, Love Nana."

I warmed the kulecha for Samantha, and she ate it.

"Nana is right here in her home, feeding me," she said. "I can taste her love."

Synchrony Singing

I want to feel the emotional fulfillment that Arabic music gives. I need to fill this void, to feel connected to my mother, my youth, my roots. The music, I know, will take me away to my parent's home. I need memories of everyday life to pour like a hard rainfall in my vision. I want to smell the aromas of my favorite foods in her kitchen, see Mom and Dad enjoying a conversation with tea in the living room, and feel the pulse of Arabic music in the background.

It's a few months since Mom died, and boxes of her most personal items are stacked up across the wall of our media room, balanced as high as we can get them. Among them are several large boxes filled with hundreds and hundreds of cassette tapes with Arabic music. All the titles are in Arabic. Years ago, Arabic-speaking family and friends copied cassette recordings of popular Arabic music to send to Mom and Dad. But I cannot read Arabic. So how to choose which cassette first?

I pop one into her old cassette player and wait for a song to play. A singer begins with a breath. I listen intently. It is a song I recognize. One singer and no music. No instruments. No background sounds. Just a smooth voice chanting, breathing and singing. Within a few notes, I feel a strong connection to the song. This song was a part of my life. I know the words. It's a love song. The voice is sweet and beautiful. As the old cassette player projects this voice from the plastic tape, I hear her.

This love song is my mother's voice singing. This is her. My mother singing. I do not know how I know this, but I am certain she was singing into her cassette player decades ago, recording a song to send to her parents in Baghdad.

I know it. This love song is for them. I understand enough Arabic to know the song is about love and missing mother and father. I begin singing along with her as she sings for her parents. Her voice is sweet and vibrant. The notes are long, beautiful.

For a time, I forget I have a body. There is nothing but our voices, both of us singing a love song to our parents, singing of how much we miss them. A timeless energy carries the notes of each word. Through this old recording of my mother's voice singing a love song from decades ago, I feel eternal perfection. This cassette, intended to travel to Baghdad, would have allowed her parents to hear her voice as if she were singing in the present. And now, today, in my present, empty with the loss of Mom, here she is, out loud, singing in this room, and I am singing with her. We are together in the present.

In the recording, overcome by her love for her parents, she begins to cry. She does not stop singing. Her voice struggles to get the notes out. I hear her inhale. Exhale. There are pauses between some of the words where the song gives way to tears.

As I sing with her, this love song to my mother, I, too, begin to cry. As best I can, I follow her notes to stay in synchrony. The beauty overwhelms me. I feel bigger than the universe. My mother's voice echoes above and beyond everything. She is here. This feels like God now. He is in every nucleus of our body, bathing us in love. Her love song, my love song. Together, we sing. My exaltation.

Epilogue

This happened the same day I was switching around three hundred TV channels and recognized a nun in a church mass from a TV station my mother watched. My mother would participate in this early morning mass from home. I never watched this station but I stopped to observe the nun praying, knowing my mother would have loved this. That same day I read in a random clip online that this same nun had died the day before. Perhaps Mom and this nun are praying together in song, too.

I Surprised Her,
She Surprised Me

Moving day. Boxes and furniture everywhere. I wish Mom were here to bless our home, to ask God for our good health and protection, happiness and love.

It's been fourteen months since she died. While I'm very excited about settling into our new home, thoughts of her infuse the day, and I miss her. My heart feels empty. I keep thinking about the day I drove her to this very spot to bless the start of our construction process. I loved her being here, watching all the action.

Earlier that morning, Jack and I had pressed rose petals and love letters into the foundation, symbolic for how much we love each other and our hope to be together for ten billion years and more. We watched the trucks pour cement onto our love letters and flowers—we'd strategically placed them where we knew they'd be under the table in my study, our bed and our bath. But what I wanted for the *whole house* was Mom's blessing.

"Mom," I'd said, picking her up at her house, "I am taking you somewhere. It's a surprise." And then we pulled up in front of the building site. It was loud. Workers everywhere. We watched the cement trucks pour the foundation. Mom was astounded to say the least. Until this moment, she knew nothing about the new house.

I guess I had been embarrassed to tell her about it. Considering our old home was lovely, I thought she might think we were crazy to build a new house. Perhaps I thought we were crazy, too. Now that it was already happening, she couldn't say, "Don't do it." Which, of course, she didn't. She did what she always did—she made the sign of the cross and she prayed.

I cherished how she sealed the house with her prayers, asking for our safety, our comfort, our faith in the future, and an increase in the flow of love and peace between me and Jack.

Now that we are moving in, I am grateful for her blessing that day, but I profoundly feel her absence. She would have been in our new home hanging out today.

I rush from room to room, trying to assemble order out of this chaos, stopping occasionally to chat with my friend and housekeeper Hannah who has flown in from Colorado to help us. As we stand in the doorway, discussing which box goes where, I hear unusual sounds coming from my phone. I've been ignoring my phone all day, but this sound is not normal, and, curious, I decide to check it. The sounds are erratic, melodic tones, as if someone is playing notes all over a keyboard, or even, perhaps, playing sounds from different instruments. What does that mean? I pull the phone out of my pocket, and freeze.

"Hannah," I say. "Hannah. Look at this."

I show her the phone. It says, "calling Mom" on the screen, and it's on speaker, making all these tones. High notes, low notes, long notes, short notes. I stare at the screen, read it over and over, "calling Mom," as these sounds blast from the phone. Hannah nods her head and looks at me, spooked. All at once, I am stunned and overjoyed, and instead of trying to make sense of my phone, I choose to focus on the message.

This is Mom's work, I'm sure of that. She has already come to me dozens of times in the last fourteen months. Though I don't know how this is happening, what I do I know is my phone never uses any of these sounds for any purpose. Plus, it was on lock mode in my pocket, and I have not been on the phone for several hours. The last time I dialed her number was fourteen months ago. It's so unlikely it could have randomly dialed her—I have over eight hundred phone numbers in my contact list. And these notes playing. Her name on the front. I will not question this intervention. I still my mind and feel the presence of God.

She is reaching out to me. That's what Mom would do, of course, give me her blessing on the first day of our move. It's exactly what would happen if she were still here in the physical realm. The rest of the day, I feel her prayers weave through everything.

Later that evening, as Jack and I are sitting at the breakfast counter eating take-out food for our first dinner in our new home, my phone makes an odd sound again. This time, it's sitting on the counter a few feet away. I grab it to see who or what it is, and the caller

ID says "Mom." All over again, she plays her symphony for Jack and me in our new home at our first meal.

Jack and I look at each other, astonished. Jack struggles for a logical explanation, but there is none. I return to my chair, this time keeping the phone near me, grateful for this timely connection with Mom as she offers us her blessings and love and makes herself known this first day and night in our new home.

Busting Open

This morning, like any other morning, I place the first of four necklaces over my head. It's a long, thin gold chain with a small oval medallion of Mother Mary that hangs very low. The other three are neatly lined up in the drawer next to each other, just as I left them last night when I took them off. I pull out the second chain, also long and gold, and pull it over my head. A simple, thin cross dangles at the end and touches the Mother Mary medallion.

The third necklace is somewhat short, but still I can get it over my head. This one is a rosary adorned in small gold beads with a very little cross at the end. The fourth is a heavy large medallion that says God on both sides and hangs from the longest, thickest chain. I tuck the four necklaces underneath my shirt and feel ready to meet the day.

Mom had to take them off when she was admitted to the hospital and changed into the hospital gown. I found them in her purse after she died.

Her necklaces touching my skin are like beams of strength. It feels good. They are no longer objects representing her faith, more symbols of my mother's energy, and they heal some of my fragility. I know how she treasured each necklace, all of them gifts to her, and she wore them for many years before her death.

I sense that when I wear them, I am capturing Mom's electric pulse stored in these medallions on chains. The charge they give off weaves her into my present, retains her in my future. And though my gut is still tight with grief, I feel blessings when I wear them.

Will the ache go away? How long will my heart suffer? It's OK, I tell myself. It's OK. I am strong and she is out there, in the heavens, where she belongs now. I search for her in everything.

Sometimes, the medallions clang together, reminding me they are there. I take them out and hold them in my hand, access her strength. Her energy was moving through these necklaces, I tell myself. Perhaps her vibration stayed in the gold and now escapes, reaches my heart, swims in my veins.

How much longer will I wear these treasures? It has been at least six months since I decided to put them on each day. Will I wear them forever? I feel some guilt in not sharing these with anyone else, Mom's treasures that slept with her. Others that love her deserve this closeness.

Mom was a giver. What would she tell me to do with them? I want them. These medallions know how many beats her heart gave each minute, felt the vibration of her breath in sleep, in prayer, at meals. But where is their home?

For now, I wear her chains, let them hang close to my heart as they did with hers. And this night, like all the other nights, I remove each necklace by pulling it over my head and placing it carefully in my top drawer, side by side with the other necklaces.

The following morning, I pick up the first one to put it over my head. The chain is loose in my fingers. The medallion drops on the floor. I pick up the medallion and chain. Surprised, I hook the chain and put the necklace on. The next necklace is the same. The clasp is unhooked. How? I don't unhook them. Never. No matter what my hair style, they always fit over my head. The third necklace is unhooked. The fourth, unhooked.

They were taken apart? What? This is not what I do. They are neat and hooked every night. How could this happen, this unclasping?

Is this God winking at me? Is it Mom? Are these necklaces part of a miracle? Is God or Mom offering a suggestion through the necklaces?

Yes. It is time, time to release the chains, and in so doing, I feel even closer to her, liberated. Again, she is my teacher, showing me how to share, to be loving and generous. The answer is here, loud and clear.

The Conversation Continues

It's been sitting on our kitchen counter for the last five days, un-opened, this small package sent in the mail. "PERISHABLE," it says in black letters. It's addressed to Jack, but he hasn't taken the time to open it. So I do. Inside? Two brownies. I read the ingredients. No. Not the stuff we eat. Just something he got in the mail from a company.

"Do you allow your children to enjoy brownies?" I ask Patty, my housekeeper. When she says yes, I hand them over to her.

As I walk away from the kitchen, a strong urge sweeps over me to go upstairs to my art studio, a place I have not been in many months. It's like a magnet, this pull, but it's not to paint. My mother's most precious belongings are in boxes in my art studio. I remember her alive and moving, singing, laughing. That was over a year ago.

The room, filled with her items, feels like a sanctuary. Still. Quiet. The boxes have been here, untouched since I carried them up the stairs shortly after her death. Inside them, there are thousands of pieces of paper with her handwriting, letters she received and old photographs. They seem eager to be seen. It's time. Time to hold her pages of writing and read her notes.

There are also two large boxes of cassettes. When I had packed them in her house, I just tossed them all in, and here they are, jumbled. Fine. I want to listen to Arabic music while I go through her belongings. Arabic music is in my blood. Listening to her music will bring the beautiful echoes of our time together to my present. Hearing the notes in the songs she played will transport me back into time. I remember how she would dance in the kitchen as she sang along and as we cooked together. She'd tell jokes. We'd laugh a lot.

But which one to choose? Mom had hundreds and hundreds of cassettes of Arabic music, most with Arabic writing on the front, which I cannot read. How will I select a cassette when I cannot read Arabic? As a surprise.

I randomly pull one out of the two boxes, then dig my hand into this large 24" x 30" box and grab for a cassette as a person would do when grabbing a ticket in a jar to win something. Then, I place the cassette into her big old cassette player, which I have kept in the box.

I'm eager to touch and smell my mother's papers, and to listen to Arabic music as we did so many times before. I am prepared to be transported. I press the play button, clueless as to what song will come out. I wait. Instead of the sounds of a velvet oud or guitar or chanting, I hear a phone ringing. An old phone. Then, a voice speaks.

"Hello?"

I recognize that voice. It's my mother. It's my mother saying hello.

"Hi Mom," I hear myself saying through the speakers. This cassette is us talking with each other! My body feels electric, thrilled. I had no idea this recording existed. I pay close attention to every tone and word in her voice as we have a conversation.

When the recording was made, I was living in Houston in an apartment not far from the house where I grew up. I was recording tutoring for a college class.

I ask Mom if she has cinnamon, spices, sugar and other ingredients at her house. I tell her I want to bake a cake.

"Bake brownies," she says, "Bake brownies like Mama Barris." Mama Barris was a sweet lady who stepped in as a second mom to my mother. She baked delicious brownies.

"No," I tell her. "Brownies are filled with sugar."

My response is ridiculous, I think, listening to myself. I was about to bake a cake! In the recording, I sound stubborn, but my mother's voice is sweet and beautiful.

I stare at the cassette player, at the same time slightly ashamed, in disbelief and wildly thrilled. Mom just told me to bake brownies. I just gave brownies to Patty twenty minutes earlier. I have not eaten brownies or handled brownies in over twenty years.

And here is her voice, alive. Her heart, beating. She is here speaking with me. Her voice is my music. I listen. I replay the conversation over and over.

This is no coincidence, finding these few minutes of my mother and myself recorded on a plastic ribbon on a cassette buried in a box with over a thousand hours of music. Her voice is timeless. Back then, this conversation was not intended to be saved. Today it is my treasure.

The Jar

It was quiet in Mom's house. For months after she died, I'd been here every day deciding the fate of all of her possessions. I worked from corner to corner, preparing her belongings to leave, including every piece of paper in her house.

After half the work was done, I began to slow down and savor just being in her home. It would soon be empty. I cherished this time, felt the stillness of her home without her. Soon the items that gave her happiness and peace would be gone from here, too.

There was one area I hadn't touched—her altar. She'd set it up in the family room on the mantle. The small area had symbolic statues of Jesus, Mother Mary and Joseph, and it included a couple of saints. She had a pale blue rosary that hung around the mother Mary statue. At her handmade alter, Mom kept a jar about four inches high, made of thick, clear glass with a heavy lid. In it, she kept holy water she received from church or from friends returning from pilgrimages.

Each morning, she said a prayer here. Once, years ago when Mom broke her wrist, I stayed with her for a month to help her, and followed her in her daily routine. We'd walk together down the hall from her bedroom to her mantle. She'd stop there, remove the lid that covered the jar, reach into the holy water to wet a finger and make the sign of the cross. After saying her prayer, she made coffee.

Mom received her daily strength from her faith in God, Mother Mary, Jesus and her favorite saints, but Mom was not the preacher type. She spoke of her faith with a boundless love and certainty, never bolstering her position.

Now, slowing down in her home, my memories of our times were played in slow motion, over and over again. I was intoxicated by the air here, inhaling air that was once in her lungs. Her presence was immensely felt.

Before turning my attention to the organizing at hand, I would sometimes imitate her ritual: I'd walk from the bedroom to her altar, imagine her wishes, know how she was praying for the protection of her family, know that she was strengthening her faith in God and praying for our faith to grow. I could almost hear Mom addressing our prayer wish list we would give her.

I found peace at her altar, felt this space conveying her faith to me, felt my own spiritual transformation growing. I relished this new-found relationship to her altar, her energy, her breath, and I'd stand there staring at the jar, knowing her fingers touched the water. Her

DNA with her prayers were in that jar. I stared and stared and stared. I dared not touch anything there.

The next week passed much the same. Every day I'd go through every room of the house, making decisions for each article. And every day I'd stare at the jar, thinking of her standing exactly here with all her awakened love, praying. Still, I dared not to touch her statues, her jar. This is her personal sanctuary, I told myself. She is leading me.

Then, one day at her altar, I noticed something that jolted me. It took me by stunned surprise. The line where the water topped in the jar had distinctly fallen to a much lower level. I had been staring at this jar for months now. The inside of the jar had many calcium rings from where the water left slight white calcium marks, so it was easy to know that the water level had been the same. It had not moved at all.

How was the water suddenly reduced? Should I doubt what I knew about this jar I've been admiring the last few months? Could I be wrong? I felt certain the water line had not moved, but maybe I was wrong.

The following day, I skipped going to her house, tied by other obligations. The next day, I entered her house to continue packing. I approached the altar with curiosity. The amount had dropped about half from two days ago. A phenomenon. I took close notice of the water line so that when I returned the following day, I could compare.

The next day, I entered the cooled, comfortable house and walked straight to the altar. There. Almost empty. Though I was afraid to touch the jar, I reasoned that I needed to pack the altar anyway. I picked up the bottle for an inspection. My fingers moved around the bottle to feel any wetness. Nothing. My fingers roamed everywhere. I felt the mantle. No wetness.

I looked closely at the jar to find any cracks or any microscopic holes. Nothing. Everything was dry. With hesitation, I lifted the jar cap. It was heavy in comparison to this small jar. The cap had a wide round brim that lay flat and fully covered the mouth of the jar.

Water could not escape from this jar top. Nothing from below. And if water were to evaporate, that would require heat and a way for the water to escape. The house was cool. Furthermore, the heavy cap fit flat and tightly on the mouth, so with heat, the water would drip back down the jar, maintaining the same amount of water in the jar.

I could not figure this out. There was no heat to cause evaporation. The jar was dry and the mantle was dry. For months, the water table had been the same. I'd observed it. I'd been staring at it every day, thinking of my mother's life and her dreams. The water level did not move. How did the holy water disappear with such abruptness? I felt as if the water wanted to be noticed. That it spoke.

I opened the jar and swirled the water. It was less than half an inch from the bottom. Then, I noticed a very tiny piece of paper floating. Though it was only the size of a sesame seed, it appeared folded up and squashed. I stared at the paper, curious how and why it got in the jar.

Alert and focused, I considered the disappearing water. I could only conclude it was a mystery. How could it diminish by 50 percent in a few days, then cut in half again in just a few more days? Could someone have taken water out of the jar?

It could have been only one person, Mom's caretaker and housekeeper. The family knew Marie Rosa well for twenty-two years, and she had a key to the house. I called her over and interrogated her about the holy water.

"No, no, no, no, no!" she said. "Me no touch anything of Ms. Mary. Me afraid. Me no touch. No!"

She continued to tell me how she respects all of Ms. Mary's items, and of course, her altar, insisting the altar items are Mary's personal religious keepsakes.

"No, no, no! I no take any water at all. I do not touch anything of Ms. Mary," she said.

I expressed to her that if she did take any water for herself, I did not mind at all, I just wanted to know. But no. She said the only thing she wanted of Mom's was her blue socks. I believed her. Plus, she was no longer going to the house since Mom's passing.

With the one possible explanation gone, I was still stymied. The water was continuing to disappear, now filling only a quarter inch in the jar. I had to travel for a week, so I locked up her house.

When I returned, I walked straight to the altar. There were ten drops left, at most. I moved the water around from one soft rounded corner to the next. The tiny paper barely moved with the drops. The next day, the water was completely gone and the tiny paper rested in a corner of the jar.

I could not figure it out. How could the amount remain static, without any movement for months, then go away in a matter of weeks? Could it be the holy water? Is her morning place of prayer so true and pure that it inspires a phenomenon that my understanding cannot grasp but my eyes can see?

A couple months later, I received a call from Tegan, a close friend of Mom's who was back in Houston from Connecticut. I suggested we have lunch at Mom's house, like the good old days, and we ate at the white breakfast table near the big windows that allow lots of light to shine in. Afterward, we walked through the house, strolling down memory lane. While at the altar, I described the details of the disappearance of water from the jar.

"It makes sense," she said. "Look at the photo above the altar." My father had put an 11" x 14" photo of me above the altar. He loved this photo—I did not realize how much until I found about ten copies of it while going through belongings.

"She is reaching to you," Tegan said, "protecting you, blessing you. It's so simple and obvious, she is reaching for you. Look at where you are. You are here. This is where you have been standing."

I nodded, accepting her explanation. However, I chose to examine the jar in front of Tegan. I removed the lid and continued talking about my lack of understanding. When I looked inside, I remembered the piece of paper. It was gone. It had not dissolved. Nor was it stuck inside the jar. It was gone. Nothing inside. The holy water, gone. The paper, gone.

Were gravity and science playing tricks on me? I believed what I was seeing and what my heart was communicating. Were these Mom's abilities to perform prayers in front of me? Were her granted wishes in tiny print and now in spirit?

After I moved her belongings out of her house, I reassembled her altar on a shelf in a closet in my house with Mom's other precious memorabilia. Although I believed the holy water mystery was to be left alone and I was convinced this was a divine action, I still wanted to experiment with the jar. I needed to know if there were a hole in it or any possible way for water to escape.

I filled the jar to a calcium mark that I could see well, almost half full. Just as at Mom's house, I stared at it. I watched it each week for about eight months. The water stayed exactly the same. No movement. It did not budge. Then I stopped. I returned a couple of months later and it was the same. Then a month later, the same. About a year after I put water in the jar, the action started.

The water level dropped about half way. Then more. This was happening. I was seeing this happen all over again. I found myself questioning why I deserved to have these blessings for me, these messages, these proofs? It was my mom who was so special, not me. I was in disbelief, however I had to believe because I was seeing this with my eyes, and I was in a peaceful and balanced state. It only took a couple of weeks for the water to drop to almost empty. Was there a message Mom was trying to communicate? Or a specific need I was focused on?

Before it dropped to almost empty, I decided to show the jar to my housekeeper, Patty, even though she knew nothing about the water disappearing from the jar at Mom's house. Patty knew the closet upstairs was hands off, and she never dusted it, nor even opened the door to the closet.

As I was explaining to Patty the water's disappearance at Mom's and now in my closet, I held the water jar on the palm of my hand. As we spoke, we looked at the jar for a good five minutes, staring at the water. Then, right before our eyes, we both saw the water fall. It dropped to another level.

We looked at each other. Patty's face became very serious. "Are we crazy?" I said. "Did we imagine it?" No. We both had to come to terms with what happened. In an instant, the water was lower. Our imaginations were not playing games.

"Yes," Patty said. "Now the water is lower. I see it higher when you showed me."

Now the water was barely covering the bottom of the jar. Was this a trick? All within seconds. How did the water escape? She and I witnessed the water disappear.

The next few days, the bottle sat as usual, on the same mirror, on the same shelf, with its lid on, surrounded by mother's prayer memorabilia. The water went away. Gone. All of it. In my cooled room. There was not one water stain on the mirror. If there were any leaks or spills, the mirror would have shown signs of it.

Was this a miracle disguised? Was this the intention? To cause me to dwell and ponder over interpretation? To arrive at the realization that God shows His miracles have no boundaries? To accept that miracles do not require explanation, though the mind longs to know how something gets from point A to point B? That Mom is spirit, formless, dimensionless, yet here?

From One Miracle
to Another

W hat on earth would I do with this?

It was a few years before Mom died. In my hands, I was hold-ing a beautiful, miniature spiral stairwell carved out of wood. Jack and I were at the house next door, paying our respects. Our neigh-bor had recently died, and his son was here hosting an estate sale. We wandered through the house, admiring items in each room, before walking to an unattached room behind the house filled with paint-ings and beautiful objects, including this small stairwell. The warm brown wood was polished and glowed. The details carved into the twenty-four stairs were meticulous.

But what would I do with it? Where would I put it? Didn't mat-ter. It was calling me, and I fell in love with it.

No, I argued with myself. I was purging. At this time in my life I was giving things away, not collecting items. This purchase was frivo-lous. I had no interest in displaying the stairs. I had no purpose for it.

Then I bought it.

Why? Sentimental value, perhaps? Since I was a girl, Mom and I frequently spoke about a stairway to heaven. And here it was. It's not that I wanted to give it to her, I just knew I had to have it. I brought it home, and when we moved, it moved with us. Then I forgot all about it, until …

It is four years later, and I'm in my art studio going through boxes of my mother's papers. The box I'm sorting now is literally up to my neck as I sit on the tile floor. There are hundreds of papers inside. I had presorted all the papers at Mom's house, right after her death, keeping anything with her handwriting on it with the intention of reviewing it later. Now is later. I pull the papers out, one by one, and stack them in piles. To the left is priority, to the right is revisit. I come across a two-page brochure on which she has written, "to Shushana and Jack, keep it, this is special and this is true." I remember seeing it before, but I'd been in too much of a hurry then to see what she'd been referencing.

When I turn the page, I see a black-and-white photo of a gorgeous wooden stairwell in a church. Is this the miniature spiral staircase I fell in love with in my neighbor's house? And where is that staircase now?

After a few moments, I recall it was placed in the corner of my studio. It must still be here. I walk across the room, push away a box, and pick up the exquisitely carved stairwell. It is identical to the one in the brochure in my hand. I read the brochure and discover that my staircase is a replica of one in an old church in Santa Fe, New Mexico. As the brochure explains, the construction of the staircase is considered miraculous, and for decades it has baffled the architects and people in the town. People make pilgrimages to see the miracle of the stairs.

And here, today, is our connection, our miracle. And here is Mom telling me it is real, instructing me to believe in miracles. She is in heaven, and here is the stairway that connects us. It is as if she knew this moment would be happening before it did and connected the dots for me. I believe her message was meant for me to see after her death, so that I would know when I take a step, she takes it with me.

This is special. And this is true.

And It Appeared

"Billy," she would say. "Billy, you need to slow down."

Billy, a quiet man, would do anything for my mother. Perhaps other people would call him a handyman. Mom called him "son." For at least fifteen years, he was at her doorstep anytime she needed anything, no matter how small the task, from changing a light bulb to getting a bell pepper from the grocery store. And every time Billy would walk out the door, he would say, "What can I do before I leave? Is there anything else?" Mother loved Billy, and with love came worry. She would lecture him, saying, "Billy, you need to take better care of your health." He was, I know, one of the most caring, important people in her life.

Since her death a few months ago, I have been going through all of Mom's belongings, carefully deciding what to keep and what to give away. In one room of my house, otherwise empty, I have stacked against the wall, from floor to ceiling, boxes of her personal belongings. It's quite a collection of boxes, eighteen feet across and nine feet high.

Two of the boxes are stuffed with letters from her friends. Others contain thousands of photographs and cards and pieces of paper in no order whatsoever, all of them sentimental to my mother. I was moving fast as I sorted, but I remember seeing a few notes from Billy on little yellow sticky papers no larger than three inches by three inches.

I've been planning to go through all these treasures from her loved ones and return them to each person that sent them. Already I've thrown out thousands of other letters from people I don't recognize, but the letters I've saved are from people like Billy, and when I return the letters, they will see how much Mom cherished them.

And so, when I ask Billy to come to my house to fix a plumbing issue in my kitchen, about a week after I've stacked the boxes against the wall, I especially wish I'd already organized everyone's cards and letters to Mom. But no. Billy's sticky notes are buried somewhere in one of those huge boxes. It will have to wait.

When Billy arrives, he immediately wants to speak of Mom, and he begins to cry. I badly wish to give Billy those tiny note papers now, now when his emotions are with her and he has tears in his eyes. This would have been the perfect time for me to have returned to him his tiny handwritten notes with his loving messages.

After we get back to talking plumbing, he wants to observe pipes in the bathroom across the house. To get there, we walk through the empty room with the boxes. As we return to the kitchen, I point to them, stacked almost to the ceiling, letting him know my task ahead to organize every one of Mom's papers.

Once Billy is resettled, I walk through the room with the boxes again. And then back. On my return, I see a tiny sheet of paper in the center of the floor. Strange. The room was spotless. I lean to pick it up so I can throw it away. The writing on it is too tiny to understand the words, so I hold it up to my eyes. "It's fixed Mom Merry, I LOVE YOU." Billy. He always spells her name "Merry," referring to her joy.

This is one of the tiny notes I saw at Mom's house and put in one of those huge boxes stuffed with the thousands of letters. And here it is? In the center of the empty floor right in my path? Right here for me to see? We did not see this before as we walked back and forth. Was it here already? How did this tiny paper appear? I *know* it was in one of the boxes against the wall. Plus, last week the floors were cleaned. This room was perfectly empty, except for the boxes placed against the wall.

I walk straight to the kitchen and give the note to Billy. He is silent.

For a while, we talk about it—the paper and Mom. I feel so connected to her, it's as if she is speaking to me. After I leave the kitchen, I am drawn to go to the large canvas bag in my study. I keep Mom's day planners in it, at least forty years of day planners. I am sensing she is guiding me to find her. I feel alert, aware that something special is happening. I grab any book and flip randomly to any page. I point, just as a kid with a globe might do when asked to pick a place on the globe to travel to, and my finger points right to Billy's name. I immediately take this old day planner to the kitchen, my finger still on his name on the page, and show Billy his name.

Mom is speaking to Billy this day. Billy knows it, and I know it, she's invoking conversations they had when she was alive.

How do we understand this power, this rearranging? Mom would say they were God's hands that placed this simple sticky note in my path, God giving us a window into His abilities, His infinite possibilities. The evidence speaks to me.

Los Angeles

The scent of lavender spills in the air. It's gorgeous. The shop I am in has a shelf filled with tester bottles of lotion. I indulge myself. The next I open is lemon with sage. Intoxicating. When I open the next jar, the aroma transports me back to a familiar place. From where do I know this scent?

The scent plays tricks with my senses. Although not a favorite, I am curiously attracted to this lotion. The scent sparks pathways in my brain, so I stand in the aisle and wait for the awareness to crystallize.

The longer I stand, the more the scent intrigues me—it is rich with complexity and change, as if one were biting into a layered cake or as if one were tasting at once all the flavors of food on a plate.

All of the smells in this one jar conspire to take me to one place. I am in Los Angeles where I was born and lived for my first five years. The scent is the family on the sofa, Steve and I playing in the living room, Mom calling me, her putting me to bed.

I dip my nose into the jar and see the house where we lived with the apple tree in front. The living room leads to the breakfast room with the bench seats on the left. The kitchen is long with a window at the end, with the stove to the right and cabinets across. The floor is black and white tile. My body is too small to reach the counters. My mother is there. The scent continues to walk me through my old house. Mom is everywhere in this scent. The house is in the jar, and she is woven into it. It comforts me—Mom passed away one year ago.

This is not her perfume from the last forty-eight years. Could it be the scent of laundry detergent Mom used back then? It doesn't matter. I don't know the flowers or herbs in the lotion, but it inspires my senses to replay scenes of my life as a very little girl. My mother is moving around our house in her fitted dress with pleats at her waist. Her skirt rustles below her knees. She is slender and smiles. Busy in the kitchen, busy in the living room.

I go to the store counter and purchase the lotion. Though it's expensive, I thrill at the way it takes me on a road trip back in time. It's therapeutic and captivating—I feel like singing and praying and loving when I open the jar and smell it. I bring it home with me to Houston and place it on the cabinet above my vanity.

I have no intention of using this for my hands, arms or legs. It has a special purpose. On occasion, I take small dabs and place it near my nose or rub it on my neck below my ears, then I am a child again with my mother. It is a magic lotion. All I do is open the jar and put my nose over it and I pass through a gate into my childhood. How can a smell whisper so many motion picture scenes? The jar has stories. It seems as if it comes to know me.

A year passes, and I continue my occasional habit of putting just a hint on my nose and neck.

I've developed a ritual. I dab my finger into the center where the lotion is lower, and with one finger I make a beautiful circular motion. Because the lotion is so thick, it stays high on the sides all around. This is the only manner in which I touch my special jar. And after all this time, there is still more than two thirds of the jar remaining.

I love to tantalize my senses with the reservoir of memories. I know what to expect and where the smells will take me. It brings me home. To my mother. Now two years after her death, the ache still lingers. I want her. Her scent. Her touch. Her breath. I reach for it on the top shelf of my vanity and bring it down to the counter. I am sitting and relaxed. I unscrew the jar to take a small dab as I did about a week ago.

I am puzzled. I quiz myself to try and remember what might have happened. Where is it? I see almost nothing in the large jar. My first thought is I must have gone insane and used massive gobs of it to cover my body. No. I know that's not true. But how can all the sides and almost the entire bottom have very little lotion remaining?

Who has been here? Where is it? For a year now, the lotion has covered the sides completely, but now there are the oddest streaks across my jar. It looks like a slaughter. Weird tracks seem to have smeared the little lotion remaining. This was not my doing, I think firmly.

My experience with the lotion has always been respectful, joyful—I feel exhilarated and happy when I remove the jar from the cabinet to use it. Now, I am confused and angry. What happened? Where is it? Today, the entire round jar has almost no lotion in it. There is only one person who would open my cabinet: my housekeeper.

No. I know her well. She would not sweep out all the lotion. And my husband has his own lotion. He would never abuse this bottle. The jar did not spill—the lotion is too thick for that, like Vaseline. Nor did it dry and shrivel up in the jar. The remaining lotion was moist anyway.

"Did you use my lotion?" I say to Patty, my housekeeper. I look her straight in the eyes. "Do you have any idea why the jar is almost empty?"

Patty is quick to say no, in no way did she use any, nor touch it.

"I am fine with you using it," I say, "or if you have taken some with you. I do not care. Just tell me."

Now Patty examines the lotion jar, puzzled as I am. She does not understand what could have happened. We laugh at the thought that I went crazy and slapped it all over me. We both know I would never do that. She examines it the way I did and gives me a curious look.

A couple of weeks go by. I take the lotion down from the place it sits and open the jar to reexamine it. It is no longer my jar of tranquility, but a puzzle unsolved. The small clumps of lotion from two weeks ago are gone. There is not enough in the large jar to keep it. Again, I show Patty the jar.

"Your mother comes to you with a force and strength," she says with a soft seriousness in her voice. "She wants you to know when she is here."

Is this Mom in her infinite world, creating intersections of our worlds? Merging all time into a timeless fusion? Are meaning and connection meant to be born from this empty jar?

I cannot see God's face, yet I can see His infinite power.

You've Got Mail

I realize sometimes it's hard to follow through with our plans, even the most important ones. And so it was at two years and five months after Mom died, I was upset with myself for not honoring the anniversaries of her death each month. I wanted to remember her at that specific time as a way to connect to her, to give her my respect.

Just after her passing, I had turned to my niece Samantha standing close by and asked, "What time is it?" I wanted to know when Mom passed. She said 2:40 p.m. That was August 13, 2014, a Wednesday.

September 13, 2014, was an emotional day. I was coming to terms with Mom's passing. At 2:40 p.m., I relived her departure. But in subsequent months, my brain skipped over the anniversaries. Every month I missed it. I tried writing it in big letters on my calendar, and still I would forget the anniversaries. The irony? I thought of her constantly. Thoughts of her life had become all consuming. And though I thought of her on the thirteenth of each month, as I did every day, I consistently missed celebrating her anniversary at the specific time.

This day, I am sitting at my desk to retrieve info from my email box. I type into the search bar "Skyhorse." My emails have a lot of stored information for Skyhorse, since it is related to my book, *The Meaty Truth*. However, instead of displaying messages for Skyhorse, the computer pulls up an email that says "Mom sick." What's going on? How does "Mom sick" relate to Skyhorse? Why isn't the search function working? I search for Skyhorse very often. It always works. Never before have I seen "Mom Sick."

And there isn't just one message. There are three, all with the same subject line. They are obvious. What is happening?

Then I see it. In the bottom right corner of the screen, I notice the time. 2:40 p.m. It's January 13. It's a Wednesday. And here is Mom, pointing this out for me. Tomorrow, I won't beat myself up for forgetting today. I say a prayer of gratitude, remember her departure and celebrate her life.

After staring at the screen, in awe for several minutes, I took photos. You will see the time at 2:43 p.m. when it dawned on me to take photos.

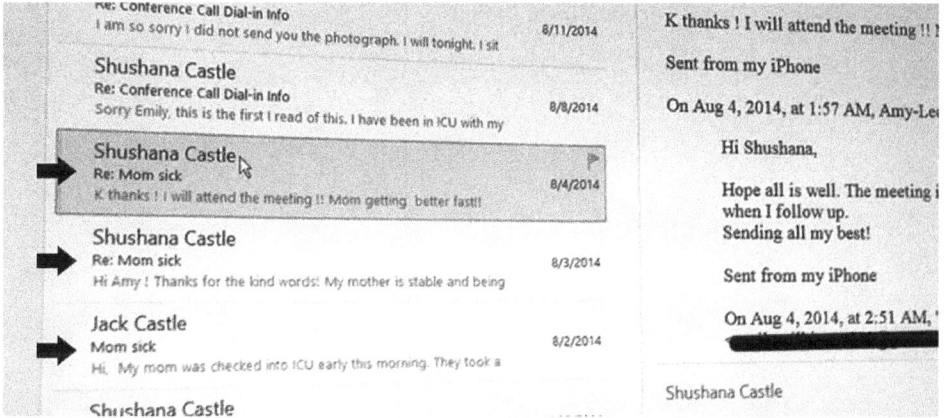

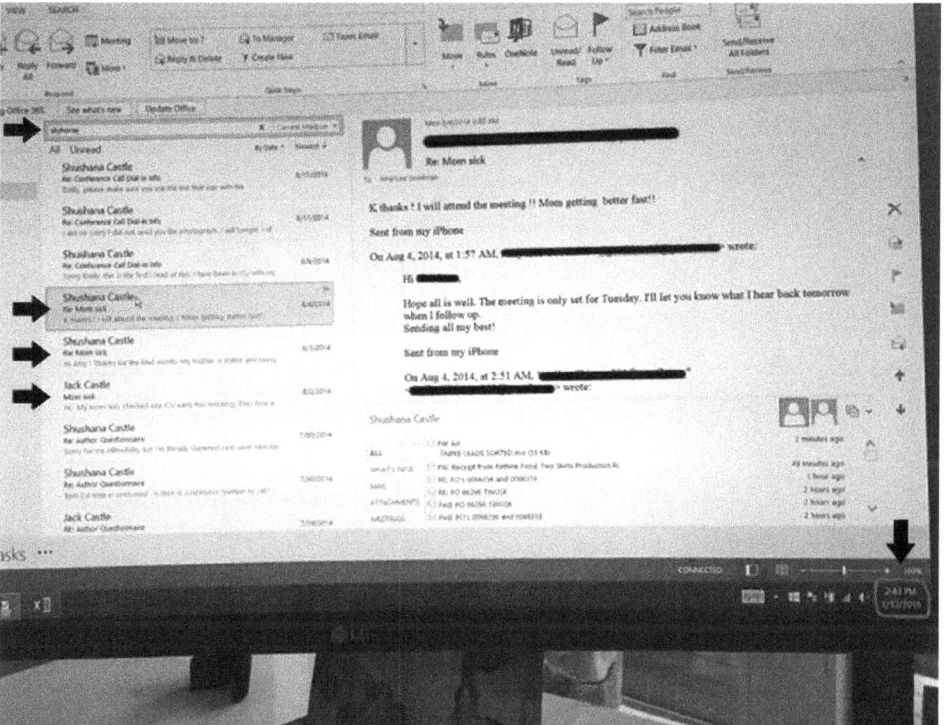

When the emails popped up I stared at them in gratitude and astonishment. Then at 2:43 pm, it occurred to me to take a photo of the screen. That photo is here.

Unmistakable

"Hi, Jack," says Samantha, just after she enters our home. Our niece looks beautiful, standing in our living room. She's five months pregnant and radiant. I turn to see my husband walking toward us from the kitchen.

"So nice to see you, sweetheart!" Jack says to her.

Samantha has just been to Medjugorje, a town in Bosnia and Herzegovina well known for its miracles. I had recently executive produced a film, *Apparition Hill*, which followed seven visitors to this sacred site where Mother Mary is said to have appeared to seven Herzegovinian children in 1981. I never would have worked on the project if my mother were still alive, but her death had been an invitation to become more spiritual, and the film was, at its heart, a spiritual conversation. Samantha brought the film to me, so I made her co-executive producer.

"Samantha has something for us, Jack," I say. "She brought you a gift."

Jack crosses the room, his arms opening. "Group hug!" he says. "All three of us!" And we step into an embrace.

"Wow," says Jack as we hug. "What's that smell? Do you smell that? It's so strong! Wow! Its smoky and heavy! It smells like that incense your Mom loved."

I do smell it.

"It's your mom," he says to me, excitement in his voice. "That smell—your mom *loved* that smell. Oud, it's called oud." He smiles as if proud of himself for remembering the name.

Mom would burn oud on very special occasions, laying the small, hard bits of wood in a little tiny dish. She'd receive this rare incense as a gift from friends and family in the Middle East, the very best oud there is. Though there are perfumes now that use it, hers was the pure wood from the heart of the Agar tree, a unique, unmistakable scent.

Jack and I inhale deeply, filling our lungs with the heavy scent. It seems as if the scent is coming from the center of the group hug.

"I *love* this scent!" I scream.

"Samantha, what perfume are you wearing?" Jack asks.

"She's pregnant," I say, "and wears no scents." I ask Samantha if her hair shampoo has scent, and she says no. Jack has a hard time believing her, the smell is so intense. But Samantha shakes her head.

And then, as we break our group hug, the scent is gone. How long was it here? It feels like minutes because the scent was so loud, but we were hugging only seven seconds or so.

So where did the scent come from? Perhaps the two rosaries Samantha brought for us? They were in her hands in the center of the group hug as we wrapped our arms around her. The rosaries, I decide, must be perfumed.

I take the little containers with the rosaries, open them and put my nose into one, then the other. No scent at all. I take out the rosaries. Smell the rosaries and again the containers. No scent. I smell Samantha. No scent.

How is this possible? Moments ago, there was a thick, heavy smoky perfume in between us and now we can't find the scent anywhere—no lingering of oud.

Then Samantha, in her grace, says, "So you understand what just happened, right, it's easy to know? Of course, Nana is coming to you with a scent. There's a conversation in these rosaries for both of you. Maybe Nana is telling you to pray," Samantha says. "The message is in the rosaries."

Yes, I think, Mom loved rosaries and prayed daily, and these rosaries were brought into our home just for us from Medjugorje. Then I am even recalling my father talking about this place.

Mom. Is this her showing me her satisfaction in the direction of my spiritual journey? Since her death, she has shown me so many examples of miracles, proving to me that the lessons of infinite love and unimaginable grace that she taught me during her life are so real. Again and again, she shows it to me. Mother Mary. I am no stranger to miracles, I grew up witnessing them often with her, but these miracles have been intimately designed for me.

Is this her way of saying she's pleased that Samantha and I are participating in the documentary, helping to spread the conversation about Mother Mary and spirituality? Is she smiling somewhere at the way every day I become more and more like her?

Epilogue One

That same day, my mother made her presence known through prominent and distinctive smells two other times. Earlier, while I was washing the dog, I kept smelling gardenias, even though it was not gardenia season. Gardenias were one of my mother's favorite flowers. I kept on lifting my head and smelling different directions to pick up the scent. Finding nothing, I'd lean back down to wash the dog. The scent was heavy, but decidedly not the oatmeal shampoo for dogs.

Washing Bella, I remembered a time when my mother said, "You spend more time with your dog than you do with me." I interpreted the mysterious gardenia scent as her way of telling me she was around.

But later that day came a more puzzling odor. I'd gone to the sink and could smell heavy cigarette smoke.

"Patty," I said to my housekeeper, "Do you smoke?" I knew she didn't.

"No, no, I don't smoke," she said.

"I smell smoke," I said, "right here. And I don't smoke."

Then, somehow through the smell, I had a vision of when I was about fifteen years old. I saw my father sitting in the breakfast room where he would smoke a couple cigarettes a day, then blow the smoke out the window. And I heard my mother tell him, "You stink. I smell good. You must stop smoking. You stink." He stopped smoking.

"I don't know why I got that message," I said, weeks later while talking to Hannah, our friend who takes care of our cabin in the wilderness in Colorado. "It doesn't make sense." I had told her about the oud and the gardenia. Both of these scents had messages I could understand. But the cigarette smoke?

"That message was for me," Hannah said. Your mother has been sending me messages to quit smoking and that is what she is saying. Your mother comes to me and helps often. That message is for me. Recently, I have been hearing her say to stop smoking. I have not smoked for one month and she is helping me."

Epilogue Two

Early one morning, I walked into Mom's house. The door is right next to the kitchen TV and the breakfast table. She was seated there watching mass, a program in another language that she loved. We waved to each other, but her eyes were glued to the screen. I saw the priest releasing incense into the church. He had a large metal container that released smoke from the incense inside as he rocked the container from a chain. I closed the door and walked past Mom. I could smell Mom had been burning incense, oud. She did it very rarely for very special occasions. The scent was so heavy at the door when I opened it up. I love that rich odor, so I walked around the kitchen to see where she was burning it.

The scent was so strong, I figured it must be here in the kitchen. No. I went into the family room searching for it. I could smell it, dense, thick, delicious. It smelled so good. I was enjoying the smell. I went back to the kitchen and took deep breaths. My clothes, I knew, would pick up the scent. I delighted in knowing she had taken out her very rare wood and burned some earlier.

It was too intense for it not to be burning now, though. How could the scent linger that long? I went into her vanity area. No trace of it. I went down the hall, to her bedroom, to the dining room and back into the kitchen. Nothing.

While Mom was still watching her mass, I sat in the kitchen to relax, absorb, inhale, and enjoy the strong scent.

"Hi, sweetheart," Mom said, when her program was over.

"Where is the oud, Mom?" I said.

"What are you talking about?" she said.

"The oud scent is everywhere. I am looking for it," I said.

"I didn't burn anything," Mom said, her eyes content.

"Mom," I said, incredulously, "Did you burn any earlier?" "No," she said. "Nothing."

"But Mom," I said, "the house is loaded with incense."

Mom pointed to the TV and said it was the mass. Then she told me that something like this had happened before. That one time the smoke in her house had been so heavy it made her cough, and it almost scared her. We stared at each other quietly, I believe both of us understanding Who was making a statement.

Unlike the other miracles I've shared, these three stories to follow show the kind of miracles that occurred with Mom while she walked the earth.

No Accident

"Shushana, I'm worried," she says.

It's Mom, calling me from her home in Houston. She's very concerned about my mother in law, Loretta, who died about a month ago.

"She is trying to tell me something, Shushana, I know it," she says. "It has something to do with her body being moved. Something about the ground. Her ground. It's going to come up. The dirt is going to move. Her body is going to move. I am sure of it," Mom says, "I cannot say it is bad or good, but this is what is going to happen, and I know it." She continues to repeat herself, "The dirt and her body are going to move."

She sounds so young on the phone, so clear, so sure of herself, like a lawyer in a courtroom, so certain of the facts. When I try to calm her down, she says, "No, no, I know what I am talking about."

When I get off the phone, I turn to our friend and home caretaker, Hannah, and say, "Mom sounds worried and concerned about Loretta."

117

I tell Hannah about how Mom said she was in her bedroom when she heard a loud boom. She got scared. She walked to the family room. There she noticed that the potted plant Loretta had given to her had tipped over. But how? The pottery was solid and heavy. There is no pet. There was no wind. The pot was next to the TV, away from any walkway. And no one was in her home except for her. The plant just fell.

But the strangest part is, I tell Hannah, that the dirt fell far away from the plant.

"There was no way the pottery could fall and have the dirt pushed so far away," Mom had said, relating to me how the dirt scattered in a line about four feet out. That's what had led Mom to reason that Loretta's dirt was going to move, her body was going to come up or move. This is how Loretta spoke to Mom.

"I will not touch the dirt and keep it the way it is, Shushana, for you to see for yourself," she had told me at the end of our phone call, knowing that in four days I was returning to Houston from Colorado.

The day after Mom's phone call, Jack receives a call from the cemetery telling him that his mother's body must come up. "They made a mistake," he tells me, his voice tight with frustration. "They only dug a three-foot hole when they put her body down. They need to dig up her grave and dig a four-foot hole."

He's very upset. "It's so wrong," he says, "that Mom is not laid to rest, not able to just settle in." Jack and I both know that Loretta would be very unhappy about this.

Three days later, I am in Houston at Mom's house, staring at the dirt on the floor. There's about four feet of spill, just as she had said. It *is* unnatural it would fall so far away from the plant. Weird. Four feet, I think. Four feet is how deep they need to dig the hole for Loretta's grave. So odd the heavy pottery could even fall over. It is clear of anything that might push it over, and Mom was in her bedroom when she heard the boom. So strange.

Though I'm astonished at Mom's accurate precognition, I also am not. This kind of event was common in my life growing up with my mom. Conversations with God, Mother Mary, angels and spirits, and her intuitions and premonitions, these were frequent. It wasn't something she tried to practice, these messages would just come to her.

Talking with Mom on the phone, I had known from experience that time would tell, and the story would unfold. Her message hadn't made sense to me because Loretta was buried. The last thing that crossed my mind is that they would dig up the earth. But Mom, she knew. She knew.

A Smiling Tree

Mom and I were always physically close—hugging, snuggling and kissing. As a little girl, I would cling to her, and on her last day, I held and caressed her face and rested on her bed with my body leaning on hers. Saying I love you and giving intimate embraces, these were part of our everyday greetings.

For decades before she died, my heart ached, wondering where her body would be placed after her death. And where would my body rest? She needs to be close to me. We must be together. Yes, I thought about these things. It pained me to think our bodies would not touch again. I wanted to be close, even after our souls have risen. It was more than just not wanting to lose myself and disappear into the soil without her. It felt bigger. It was an empty hole with sadness in my life that I cannot explain. This focus pulled on me. However, I never addressed buying a gravesite. It did not occur to me. I never planned for my burial place, nor hers.

Then my father died. We had no gravesite for him. The next day, my brother Steve told my mother and me that he would make all the arrangements for the funeral and burial services, from start to finish, and for Dad's celebration party afterwards. I was grateful, because I could not emotionally handle the selection of our Dad's burial site.

Because he still had to work at the office and had family responsibilities while making all the arrangements, Steve's personal assistant of many years, whom he trusted, was asked to find gravesites that day for Mom and Dad in a cemetery that Mom selected.

Steve's assistant met with the gravesite manager, who drove her through the eighty-eight acres of this vast and wide cemetery in a golf cart. She narrowed the choices of her liking to three ideal locations.

The cemetery had many trees, including areas of the cemetery that were newly developed and less expensive. His assistant fell in love with a tree that provided shade right next to a plot for two people. It was on a small hill. She recently told me the other plots were equally beautiful in their location, however this tree spoke to her.

She recommended that spot to Steve, and though Steve never saw the plots, nor did he go to the cemetery, he took her recommendation and wrote the check for the two places, grateful for her assistance.

Now it's a few days later. We've just been to my father's funeral at the church, and our whole family is gathered in the cemetery to bury my father. The grandchildren, Mom and the rest of the family are at Dad's gravesite, praying. I am sitting in a chair several feet away from where my father will go down. There is a place next to his plot that will be for my mother. It is an odd feeling seeing this land.

As I look around, it hits me. I cannot believe what I am seeing—the grave of my husband's father. The tree that Steve's assistant admired grows between my parents' plot and Jack's parents' plot. That's the land where Jack will be buried and where I will be buried next to him. Mom and I will be next to each other!

My sorrow and pain for my father's death is layered with a growing happiness and relief that my burial place will someday be next to my mother's. Right where my eyes are staring.

I have to tell my mother—we speak openly about death. I catch her eye, whisper in her ear and point to where I will rest someday. Mom's expression is both stunned and excited. Her eyes brighten and her mouth opens. Even on this sad day, there is great joy in this miracle. We will share this soil.

Fifty feet of space separates the plots. The tree with big branches and leaves that shades my parents' land every season will be between us. We will share the same tree roots deep in the earth, the same birds singing, the same soil and rain runoff.

We were so close while Mom walked the ground, and now the comfort of knowing we will be together below has been granted to me. Prayers answered.

Because She Asked
Me To

I've been sitting in his room for at least six hours. The room is silent. I cannot even hear him breathe. I haven't moved except to touch his hand, very gently so as not to wake him. I softly keep my hand over his, feeling his warmth, thanking him for everything he has taught me and given me throughout my life. I know his end is very near, at least as we know life on earth.

Dad's bed is centered in the middle of the room, and a big window covers one of the walls. There's a garden out the window, and a bright light that shines all night long that brings a warm glow to the room and my father's face.

I've had nothing to drink so that I won't have to go to the bathroom. I sit on the chair next to his bed, as still as possible so as not to disturb him nor wake him. I want to be with him when he departs from this physical world, when his soul moves on. It's my last way of saying thank you.

Just a few weeks ago, we were talking about the stock market and God. But that was before my father began refusing food. Maybe even after he refused food. Three days ago, he stopped accepting the gelatin drink, a water made thick so he won't choke. When he began refusing his fluids, that's when the truth began pulling at my heart.

It's not a surprise. I've been watching him become increasingly fragile over the years, refusing kidney dialysis to deal with natural aging symptoms. For a long time, he still functioned just fine without it. Now, at eighty-two, he's his frailest ever.

Mentally, however, he's still been sharp and clever and wise in his advice. He did, after all, study and have degrees psychology, business and theology at prestigious universities, and he was always obsessed with books. His muscles were naturally always huge and chiseled even without working out, but I've watched as his limbs turn to skin and bones. Now he is so weak he cannot speak.

I feel it again.

I've been living it each day over the last few days, this physical pressure, as if magnets are trying to pull me down. There is something that is trying to crush me in this room. I almost can't breathe. I feel as if there are thousand-pound weights on my chest. If I had to describe it, I'd say this pulling was trying to stop my heart. I don't understand this sensation.

Despite the feeling, I stay, though I am certain Dad does not need me here. His primary relationship is with God. He has never been dependent on people, it seems. It's as if all of his life he has prepared himself for heaven. He was a practicing Deacon in the Catholic Church. He served the Holy Eucharist during mass. He is not afraid of death, this I know for certain. I am the one that wants to be here, close to my father when he passes.

For now, he is profoundly calm in his bed. I decide to leave for the night. My tennis shoes make no sound. My body makes no sound. I try not to move the air, concentrating on every motion, every step I take as I get up to leave so as not to make any sound whatsoever, and I am very successful.

As I close the door behind me, the door is completely silent, not even a click. Nothing. Then, I stand outside the door and contemplate how this might be the last time I see my father alive. I don't want to leave. For a moment, standing at the door, I don't want to move. I wish time could stand still. There is a heavy sadness. I grapple with whether I should leave or stay. I decide to open the door again. As I open the door, the light from outside the bedroom allows me to clearly see him lying on his bed. But something is very different.

As I fully open the door, I see his right arm has already been lifted up, stretching out from the bed as if he is reaching for someone. He was so weak and in such a deep sleep the whole time I was in the room, for hours and hours, and now he's so able? I see his arm in the air fully extended, his long, beautiful fingers curling into the palm of his hand. As if in slow motion, his hand turns and I see his elbow now bending. He gently returns his hand to the bed, but this time not straight by his side. This time, he lets his hand rest on his heart.

He did not move at all the entire time I was in the room, and now the thirty seconds I was outside of his room he extends his arm above his body high above his hips?

I stay in the hall and slowly close the door. This is not for my eyes to see. I am not privileged. I feel as if I have trespassed and violated his personal time with God and self. I am not supposed to see this. He was waiting for me to leave. In fact, he seemed not at all interested in my mother and me the last few days when we went to visit him. His interest has been in prayer.

The next day, Mom and I visit my father. He's so feeble he does not acknowledge us, nor does he seem to notice we are here. His hands lay peacefully on his chest. Mom and I sit beside each other and watch as his lips move in prayer. Though we hear almost no sound, we see his lips moving reciting the Lord's Prayer, the Hail Mary, and other prayers he taught me when I was a girl. He's saying them in Aramaic, his original tongue. We are in awe of this man praying alone in such a state of grace.

I say nothing to my mother about this strong pulling on my body as if I will be smothered. It's quite different from an emotional drain—I know what that feels like. And this is not it. In fact, I feel emotionally, mentally strong. But this pulling is wearing me out. It seems to be back again, here in this room, an overwhelming physical presence. It feels as if it will crush me, as if it is trying to suck me away. It is something beyond our humanness. I do not know what it is at the time, but I feel it draining me.

Mom and I sit together, watching him pray, staring at him. He seems asleep. Then, after thirty minutes, Mom and I begin to softly speak to each other. My father turns his head to the right, opens his eyes and yells at us.

"*Se!*" he cries, his voice forceful and clear. It means *go* in Aramaic. He tells us with a strong voice to leave. But we stay anyway.

Instead, Mom and I give each other a knowing look. Neither of us want to leave. We stay perfectly still so that he thinks we have left. After another half hour, he looks up and begins speaking in Aramaic. His voice is strong—it's the voice of my father that I remember, a voice I haven't heard in many months.

He is calling to his sister. "Mosha! Hurry up," he says, in Aramaic. "Come and get me." And then he calls out to his mother, "Yumma! What is taking you so long? Hurry! Hurry!" His eyes are big, looking up over his hips. He seems impatient. A bit angry almost. "Come on," he says, "what are you doing? Hurry up!" all in Aramaic.

Dad continues to stir, restless in his bed, then puts his hands up in the air as if to summon his mother and sister.

Mom and I look at each other, stunned, slightly freaked and in disbelief. We know we need to get out of the room. We have no business being in here. This is his spiritual time. We know he does not want us here, he told us so when we disrupted him earlier. We get up right after we witness this. Mom walks to his side.

"I love you," she says, her voice tender and strong. "I love you." She cries. She knows.

"Dad," I say, "I love you." He pays no attention to us. He shows no acknowledgement.

I consider he may be remembering a time with his sister and mother, perhaps returning to his youth. But something in me knows he is seeing something new, something out of the scope of memory, something outside of his body. It feels tied to the weighty presence.

Mom and I leave the room and close the door. A few hours later, he leaves to be with his sister and mother.

Days and weeks later, Mom and I discuss this tugging sensation in his room. I tell her about the feeling I'd had as I was sitting with him—the pull, the weight, the tug. Each time I left the room it still lingered with me for a while. I would still feel it in my body. I'd feel mentally strong and physically exhausted.

"I felt it too," Mom says, "I could not take it anymore, I just had to leave." Mom and I were flabbergasted that we both felt it.

We describe it to each other as if it were trying to stop our hearts and crush us. There was a profound sense that we did not belong in the room. We both agree, it was like "a physical pressure," as Mom says. "It felt as if it were trying to take me, as if I were going to die."

We're both stunned that the other had the same experience. We wonder, was it God? Or angels? Or spirit? We were confident the energy was directly related to helping Dad pass to the afterlife.

It is eleven years later when I am sitting in my bed, my husband asleep beside me. I am on my computer, typing the last story of how my mother has come to me after her physical death. Things become blurry in the room, and Mom comes to me. In a voice that is not a voice, she tells me to tell the story of my father's death.

Dad's intimate experience? It was serene and peaceful and meant only for him. I am very reluctant. That is his private experience. He is not asking me to share what my mother and I witnessed.

Yes, she says, Dad's story. My intuition and her voice tells me she wants me to share how real the force was in the room, how intensely that powerful tug that was pulling on us, and that Dad really did have an actual communication with his sister Mosha and his mother. That him calling out to them to hurry up came not from a memory but from an interaction with a realm she and I could not then see. This must be the only reason why she would ask me to include Dad's story.

And so, though I do not want to trespass on Dad's privacy, though I know it would not be his wish for others to know of his final experience here on earth, Mom and I watching God and his spiritual family receiving him, I tell my mother reluctantly that I will include it. I never imagined I would tell his personal story in a book.

Epilogue

A couple of weeks before Dad passed, I asked him for advice around attending an international water conference in New York. We were in Houston at the time. I told him about my career transition into the water industry after twenty-plus years of working in the financial securities sector. I had returned to school and earned a master's degree in environmental management and water, and some of the icons that inspired me would be at this conference. He urged me to attend and told me to do what makes me happy and what feels right for my career. He was emphatic and sincere.

As it was, the conference took place soon after my father's death. My mother thought it was important for me to attend and gave me her blessing. All the who's who in the international water world were speaking, and I had read all their articles and books. She knew how much it mattered to me and encourage me to fly to New York.

On the first day of the conference, five speakers who were my water world icons were to speak. Because of my flight, I missed the morning session. It was lunchtime when I arrived at the conference, but I delayed going in—I chose instead to speak at length to several relatives who called to offer their condolences. I missed the talk by my most favorite water expert during the first half of the luncheon.

By then, I almost regretted that I had flown to New York. As it was, I walked into the luncheon with the place packed and all the tables full. There must have been over eight hundred people in the lunch room. I walked through the room, not able to find a seat. People had already started on their main course. Then, across the room, I saw someone wave to me, pointing to an empty seat at their table.

I walked all the way to it. As I sat down, I felt as if I recognized the person greeting me. Everyone at the table stopped their conversations to say hello and introduce themselves. It happened to be the VIP reserved table with all the main speakers and most influential people in the room—the very people whom I had shown up to see were seated to my left, to my right, and all around the table. They were passing their cards to me and I had the chance to engage in conversation with each one of them.

It was more than I could ask for. It was my father, I thought, and God, who had a hand in bringing me to exactly the right table.

Even Now: In Your Face Evidence, Mom Shows Me Twice

This morning, I woke with a calm feeling. I've accomplished what my mother asked of me—I've shared the stories she delivered. It's a strange and satisfying feeling, this completion. The endeavor was not easy, *and* it was a total joy and privilege. Writing the miracles has doubly blessed me, allowing me to think about my mother every day as I've worked on the book.

As of this morning, however, I still had a few decisions left to make, especially concerning the book cover. I knew I wanted there to be blue—blue is Mom's favorite color. But which of the hundreds of shades of blue to use? Blue with a little green in it? Sky blue? Navy blue? What shade would she most love? The blue on Mom's Mother

Mary statue that she touched every morning? I wanted the blue to be her favorite.

So, this morning, I spoke about it with Susan, my sister in love.

"Use any blue," she said. "Mom would love any blue."

But I could not accept that. The book needed to have the *right* shade. *Her* blue. I spoke to my dear friend Virginia about blues. Still, I couldn't decide.

Perhaps because I was nearing the end of the book project, I felt separated from Mom. I decided to go to her gravesite. I hadn't been there in a couple of months since before Hurricane Harvey. Experts called this hurricane a one-in-five-hundred-years kind of event. After Harvey, much of Houston was underwater, including the cemetery, which was closed for two weeks.

I arrived at her gravesite to find peace and to slow down, knowing I can do that there, and as I approached her ground I saw something bright—a small round ball. A bright, beautiful blue! On her grave! One of her favorite blues! And the ball was right above where her left palm is. Mom was left handed. She clearly was showing me what color blue.

The tiny floating ball might have traveled for days and many miles, but it came to land in the space right above the left palm of her hand. I looked around the grave. There was no trash, no debris anywhere. I walked around the cemetery for ten minutes to see if I could find any other debris. Nothing. Just the blue ball. I drove around the vast cemetery. Eighty-eight acres, clean.

And so it is Mom who chose the color blue for her book—the color you see on the front cover—just as she gave me the thirty-plus miracles you've read (and at least twenty five more that I haven't written about). I know she is telling me, we got this. Trust in life after life. She is telling me these dimensions merge into one. She is here, making herself present. The miracles are unfolding once again.

This was no coincidence. The ball is the earth with its turquoise water that appears so small in her palm. And she is so big. Like infinity. Like the universe. She is holding and caring for the earth.

I returned home with the blue ball as a souvenir. Then, as has happened before, I had the feeling that I was being led, that my hands were not my hands. I had loads to do, but for whatever wild purpose, I stood on my rolling chair to reach a top shelf in my study. I was aware it was not a smart idea, and I was also aware that I had no cause, no purpose, for looking on that shelf.

I found a little box in the back in which I keep memorable business cards from the 1990s. I quickly flipped through them without knowing why.

There, I found a card with an image of Saint Therese de Lisieux with the dates December 7-8, 1999. Mom was born December 8. I had taken her to pay her respects to Saint Therese de Lisieux when the saint's body toured Houston on December 8, 1999. This was the saint I had included in an epilogue earlier in this book. So, I thought, this is how this connects. But I did not yet know the half of it.

Later tonight, Jack and I visited our niece and her husband, Samantha and Connor, and their six-day-old baby, Andrew. I told them the story of the turquoise ball and showed them the photo. They were amazed and called it "a Nana miracle." I responded, "It's a Nana thing, a God thing."

Then, immediately out of nowhere, Samantha told me to pray a nine-day novena to Saint Therese de Lisieux.

Saint Therese de Lisieux? I have never heard Samantha say that name before. And why would she have brought it up? We were talking about the turquoise ball. Was it a Nana whisper?

Then she added, "Novenas are known for prayers being answered. Nana was always praying novenas for people's wishes." Yes, I think, I remember Mom often doing that.

Returning home, I went straight to my computer and picked up the Saint Therese de Lisieux card that I had left beside it. I stared at Saint Therese, then turned the card over in my palm, and was stirred and moved by her words on the back of the card. Nine words. I was certain Mom and Saint Therese had chosen them to be the last nine words in the book:

"I will spend my Heaven doing good upon earth."

About the Author

Author, environmental activist and producer Shushana Castle worked for over twenty years structuring and trading fixed income securities in the international financial markets. She traveled the world extensively, originating tens of billions of dollars in financial instruments for tier-one portfolios. She ranked number one worldwide for several years in her specialty field.

She left Wall Street and used her financial experience to help raise capital for nonprofits that help empower women in developing countries. She went on to earn a master's degree in environmental management and water. She now presides on numerous environmental boards.

Driven by a passion to improve our environment, Castle produced a monthly one-hour TV show for public television, in which she interviewed experts in the medical and environmental fields. She also hosted a monthly public radio show, delivering solutions to critical environmental issues. She now produces documentaries on the environment, social issues and animal rights and has co-authored two books: *Rethink Food: 100 Plus Doctors Can't Be Wrong* and *The Meaty Truth*.

Though Castle was raised in Houston, her parents always emphasized her Chaldean roots and raised her speaking Aramaic in the home, a language now spoken by only one and a half million people worldwide. Her mother urged her to volunteer her services, thus Shushana was involved for years teaching homeless teenagers, young adults without eyesight and women in conflict.

She's an avid mountain hiker, sports enthusiast and animal lover. She and her husband divide their time between Texas and Colorado. She loves to cook and has three wonderful adult stepsons.

Acknowledgements

My darling Jack, I love you. Thank you for your love and support that is bigger than the Universe. I am so blessed you are in my life. Lean on me.

My fabulous editor, Rosemerry Wahtola Trommer, who beautifully constructed my writing. I am forever grateful.

My brother Steven who always showered Mom and Dad with endless love and attention, thank you.

Mom

—Shushana Castle, Oct. 24, 2017

Mom, you are but one wave,
God is the ocean.
You sing to the winds and tide,
a sweeping caress, the shore changes.
How did you pick up so gracefully
the shipwreck marooned on shore,
returning it to the deep blue, it calls home?
Dancing with each grain of sand,
holding the rocks,
such a fluid welcome
into the reaches of the ocean.
Drowning in faith.
Discovering authentic love.
Swimming in Spirit.
Filling the ocean
one by one, two by two.
Who are you,
breathing deep in the ocean?
The wave guides, and
returns again and again.
The sun sets.
The moon lights.
The stars call.
Again, holding the rocks,
the sand, the shipwrecks,
all those people you carry
with heavy hearts—the shattered, the searching.
And the wave disappears, into the ocean,
swallowed in love.
Bound to Heaven.
Mom, the Ocean reflects in your Face!
It is time.
Go.

Mary Maizy Kherkher **Dec. 8, 1932—Aug. 13, 2014**

Her Loving Husband
Razouk Mansour Kherkher Jan. 16, 1924—Nov. 6, 2006

Her Loving Parents
Habbuba Sinawi Maizy July 1, 1902—Sept. 11, 1988
Yousif Maizy July 1, 1895—Nov. 25, 1976

Her Loving Sisters
Hassina Maizy Bahrou April 8, 1928—Aug. 9, 2005
Georgette Maizy Tobia July 14, 1936—April 12, 2006
Samira Maizy Sinawi Feb. 28, 1941—

Her Loving Brothers
George Yousif Maizy Sept. 27, 1927—Oct. 28, 1998
Louis Yousif Maizy Jan. 1934—Feb. 23, 1958
Manuel Yousif Maizy Oct 1, 1937—
Samir Yousif Maizy Nov. 1943—

www.ingramcontent.com/pod-product-compliance
Lightning Source LLC
Chambersburg PA
CBHW061725020426
42331CB00006B/1095